THE GLOBAL
ENVIRONMENT

STEPHEN STERLING

SUE LYLE

This book may be used in conjunction with the television series produced by the International Broadcasting Trust (IBT) for BBC Schools TV. The authors and publishers would like to thank Edwina Vardey (Series Editor, IBT) and Len Brown (Executive Producer, Schools TV) for their cooperation.

Thanks are also due to the following for their financial support in the production of the TV series and accompanying printed materials.

The World Wide Fund for Nature
The Commission of the European Community
Oxfam
The Nature Conservancy Council
The Overseas Development Administration
The Department of the Environment
The Norwegian Agency for Development Cooperation

IBT is an educational charity and an independent production company producing films and printed materials on development and environmental issues. For further information, please write to: IBT, 2 Ferdinand Place, London NW1 8EE (tel: 071 482 2847).

The Global Environment is printed on paper produced by Papyrus Nymölla, an environmentally friendly paper mill. The paper pulp is non-chlorine bleached so that cancer-causing dioxins, once associated with the process, are not produced. The mill uses carefully managed forests and recovers 97% of all chemicals used.

Edited by **Lynette Aitken**, IBT
Cover and book design by **Amanda Askwith**
Picture research by **Helen Taylor**
Illustrated by **Sue Henry, Mike Gilkes** and **Oxford Illustrators Ltd**
Editorial management by **Kay Hyman**

PUBLISHED BY BBC EDUCATIONAL PUBLISHING AND LONGMAN GROUP UK LIMITED

BBC Educational Publishing
a division of
BBC Enterprises Limited
Woodlands
80 Wood Lane
London W12 0TT

Longman Group UK Limited
Longman House
Burnt Mill
Harlow
Essex CM20 2JE
England and Associated Companies throughout the world

First published 1991
Second impression 1992
© BBC Enterprises Ltd/Longman Group UK Ltd 1991
Illustrations © Sue Henry; Mike Gilkes; Oxford Illustrators Ltd
Set in 12/14 pt Meridien Roman
ISBN 0 582 07417 7
Typeset by Ace Filmsetting Ltd
Colour origination by Daylight Colour Art
Produced by Longman Singapore Publishers Pte Ltd
Printed in Singapore

Acknowledgement is due to the following, whose permission is required for multiple reproduction:
Greenprint for the extract on p8, adapted from *The Race For Riches* by Jeremy Seabrook; **Oxfam Education** for the extract on p11, adapted from *Concejo*; **Verso** for the extract on p19, adapted from *I, Rigoberta Menchù*, edited by Elizabeth Burgos-Debray, and for the extract on p34, adapted from *The Fate of the Forest: developers, destroyers and defenders of the Amazon* by Susanna Hecht and Alexander Cockburn; **Oxfam Publications** for the extract on p21, adapted from *Burkina Faso: New Life For The Sahel?*; **New Internationalist Publications** for the extract on p27, adapted from 'A Well Woman'.

The publishers have made every attempt to trace copyright holders, but in cases where they may have failed will be pleased to make the necessary arrangements at the first opportunity.

Picture credits

Aspect Picture Library page 10 (top); **Barnaby's Picture Library** 60 (top R Rixon); **The British Petroleum Company** 47 (above and bottom right), 59 (right); **J Allan Cash Ltd** 6, 13; **Centre for Alternative Technology** 47 (middle); **Christian Aid Photo Library** 73 (bottom S Franklin), 84 (bottom S Franklin); **Ecoscene** 14 (Nicholis), 26 (top Harwood), 30 and 31 (top S Morgan), 55 (bottom left Hawkes), 65 (top S Morgan), 67 (top Harwood and bottom Whitty), 68 (S Morgan), 75 (bottom Harwood), 84 (top), 86 (bottom J Meech), 89 (S Morgan); **The Environmental Picture Library** 17 (top H Girardet), 47 (top A Olah), 55 (top), 63 (R Brook); **Greenpeace** 44 (top Vennemann), 77 (Walker); **Grant Heilman Photography** 16 (top A Pitcairn); **Holt Studios Ltd** 17 (bottom) and 18 (N Cattlin); **Hutchinson Photo Library** 11, 19, 20 (B Regent), 31 (bottom), 33 (top); **ICCE Photo Library** 49 (M Boulton), 55 (bottom right D Blow), 60 (bottom C Agrew), 62 and 66 (Rob Cousins), 86 (top M Boulton), 88; **Donald Innes Studios** 73 (top); **Intermediate Technology** 51; **IBT** 8, 58, 59 (left); **IPPF** 85 (bottom Jeremy Hamand); **Methodist Church Overseas Division** 78; **Milton Keynes Development Corporation** 53; **NASA** back cover; **National Power** 50; **Network Photographers** 9 (top B Lewis and bottom J Sturrock), 25 (J Hartley) 26 (bottom), 87 (J Hartley); **Panos Pictures** 7 (R Giling); 10 (bottom D Reed); 16 (bottom), 21 (J Hartley); 24 (R Berriedale-Johnson), 42 (T Bolstad), 48 (A le Garsmeur), 61 (L Taylor), 68 (bottom R Giling), 75 (top H Bradner), 76 (A le Garsmeur), 80 and 81 (J Hartley), 82 (D Reed), 85 (top Copper and Hammond); **Philips Lighting** 44 (bottom); **Planet Earth Pictures** 71 (P Scoones); **Powergen** 47 (bottom left); **Science Photo Library** front cover, 22, 38, 54; **South American Pictures** 33 (bottom T Morrison); **Still Pictures** 27 and 35 (M Edwards); **Varta** 65 (bottom); **Water Aid** 29; **WWF** 28 (B Chapman), 31 (middle C Harvey), 34 (E Parker), 37 (F Sullivan); **Yanesha Forestry Co-operative** 36.

SYMBOLS

Activity

Things you can do yourself
to help the environment

Words in *italics* are explained in the Glossary, page 94.

Contents

Countries featured in this book

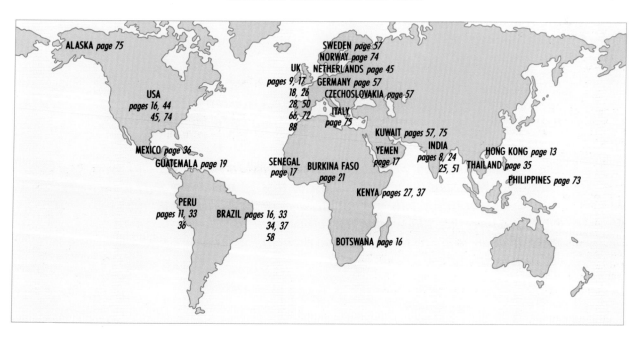

ALASKA *page 75*

SWEDEN *page 57*
NORWAY *page 74*
UK   NETHERLANDS *page 45*
pages 9, 17   GERMANY *page 57*
18, 26   CZECHOSLOVAKIA *page 57*
28, 50   ITALY
66, 72   *page 75*
88

USA
pages 16, 44
45, 74

KUWAIT *pages 57, 75*

MEXICO *page 36*
GUATEMALA *page 19*

YEMEN   INDIA
page 17   *pages 8, 24*
25, 51

HONG KONG *page 13*
THAILAND *page 35*

SENEGAL   BURKINA FASO
page 17   *page 21*

PHILIPPINES *page 73*

KENYA *pages 27, 37*

PERU
pages 11, 33
36   BRAZIL *pages 16, 33*
34, 37
58

BOTSWANA *page 16*

This is...the global environment

It took us, the human species, around three million years before we could take this photograph from space of our home—the planet we call Earth, which we share with millions of other species. Everything we care about is here.

Astronauts who have seen the Earth from space have been struck by its beauty, and by the thought that everything on it is interconnected. These are some of the things that astronauts have said:

Sultan Bin Salman Al Saud (from Saudi Arabia):

'The first day or so, we all pointed to our countries. The third or fourth day, we were pointing to our continents. By the fifth day, we were aware of only one Earth.'

John David Bartoe (from the USA):

'As I looked down I saw huge forests extending across several borders, and I watched the extent of one ocean touch the shores of separate continents. Two words leap to mind as I look down on all this. Commonality and interdependence. We are one world.'

Close your eyes and imagine you are an astronaut. When you open them again, imagine you are looking through the window of your space capsule and seeing the picture on this page for real. What thoughts do you have?

Compared to the planet, which is billions of years old, the human species is very young. But we have quickly made our mark. Imagine that the whole of Earth's history had happened in the last 100 years . . .

The dinosaur came and went about one year ago. People arrived only two weeks ago. We began the widespread use of fossil fuels at the start of the industrial revolution only five minutes ago. In these brief five minutes we have upset more than ninety-nine years of development of the Earth's environment. If we are to protect the climate and environment for future generations, we need to act in the next four seconds.

Indigenous peoples such as rainforest dwellers and Native Americans have known over thousands of years that people must care for their environment if they are to survive. Here's a famous statement that the American Indian Chief Seattle made over 100 years ago:

'The Earth does not belong to man, man belongs to the Earth. All things are connected. Whatever befalls the Earth befalls the sons of the Earth. Man did not weave the web of life; he is merely a strand in it. Whatever he does to the web, he does to himself.'

Now, Chief Seattle's warning seems to be coming true.

Pollution is found worldwide, unique environments such as the rainforests are being destroyed, around fifty plant and animal species are made extinct every day. In some places, soil is turning to desert and, in others, rain is becoming acid. The global climate is changing and many millions of people live with daily poverty and hunger.

What is going wrong? Unfortunately, there is no simple answer. Many things contribute to the situation the global environment is now facing.

This book takes you on a brief journey through some key issues—it looks at how the environment works, how we are causing problems, and how these can be tackled at local, national and global levels.

Each chapter starts with a challenge and an investigation for you to undertake. You will not find all the answers in the book—but it should set you thinking and acting to help the environment!

The big challenge for all the Earth's people is to find ways of 'living more lightly on the planet': ways that do not cause environmental damage, and that will allow the Earth to support generations to come. This is what the book is about.

▶ How can we treat the planet, our home, in a more *sustainable* way?

Let's start our journey by coming down to Earth, and looking at the local home of nearly half the world's population—the city.

Coming down to Earth!

The chances are that you live in a town or city. If so, you'll see buildings and streets every day. That's your local environment. But imagine you were seeing the Earth from deep space— you'd get a very different view. There's something that may well surprise you—you wouldn't be able to see the effect of people on the Earth at all!

As you approached the Earth's surface, the first thing you would see, if it were dark, would be the clusters of lights from cities and flares from natural gas. As you got nearer, you'd begin to see huge centres of population, spread over every continent except Antarctica. In these towns and cities, you would find over two-fifths of the population that inhabits the planet.

A tale of two cities

▶ Look at the pictures opposite and describe the similarities and differences. Where do you think each of the pictures was taken?

Most cities can boast great achievements—in architecture, art, music, poetry—and a comfortable lifestyle for many of their people. But not everyone shares in the benefits of city life. Sprawling round the edges of expanding *Third World* cities are the many *shanty towns*, where people often live without basic services like water and sanitation. In the shadow of the smart new office blocks of Europe or the United States, you will often find the poverty of inner-city slums. Two cities and two lifestyles exist alongside each other.

Cities not only affect the local environment. Because they use materials from almost any part of the world, they often affect even very distant environments. You will find that aspects of all the topics you read about in this book are related to the growth of cities around the world.

THE CHALLENGE

▶HOW CAN CITIES BE MADE BETTER TO LIVE IN, AND HAVE A LESS HARMFUL EFFECT ON THE ENVIRONMENT?

YOUR INVESTIGATION

▶WHY ARE CITIES EXPANDING, PARTICULARLY IN THE THIRD WORLD?

▶WHAT PROBLEMS DO CITIES BRING?

▶WHAT SOLUTIONS MAY THERE BE?

Above: *sunset in Chicago, USA*

The urban population is the population that lives in cities. As more people live in cities, we say that the population is becoming urbanised. Look at the graph.

The term 'more developed regions' refers to those countries that have been developing their industries over the last two hundred years or more. They are often called the *industrialised* countries. 'Less developed regions' describes countries that have little industry or have only begun to industrialise this century. Many of them supply *raw materials*, like cotton, coffee or copper, to the industrialised countries. The majority of the people are often very poor. These countries are sometimes referred to as the Third World.

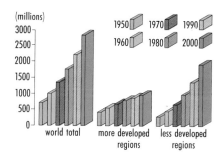

Urban population growth

 ▶What does the graph show you? Why are the patterns of urban growth different?

Why do cities keep growing?

There are three main reasons for urban growth. One is the natural increase in local population. Every day there are a quarter of a million more people on Earth than the day before. Another reason is that people move into the towns from surrounding areas or more distant places. This is called migration. The third reason is that nearby rural areas become part of the city as it spreads outward.

▶Investigate the growth of your local or nearest town or city since 1800. Have each of the above reasons been important? When?

▶Draw a bar graph to represent the figures on the right relating to London and Mexico City. What do they show about population growth?

CITYFACTS

▶Most large cities in the Third World are growing much faster than those in the industrialised countries ever did.

▶In the year 1801 the population of London was 1.1 million; in 1901 it was 6.6 million.

▶The population of Mexico City was 3 million in 1950, 20 million in 1990.

▶By the year 2000, nearly half the world's population will live in towns or cities.

▶By that time, over two-thirds of the world's largest cities will be in the Third World.

Welcome to the city!

When cities in Europe began to expand during the nineteenth century, it was during a time when new wealth was being created. This meant that there was money available to put into building *infrastructure*—houses, roads, transport, drainage, sewers, schools, etc. Today, in the countries of the Third World, cities are growing much faster, but without the money to build an adequate infrastructure.

 ▶As you read the following description, imagine you are walking through Dharavi, a slum of Bombay, in India.

Although Dharavi doesn't appear on the official map of Bombay, it has long been known as the largest slum in Asia. But, if it is Bombay's shame, it is also a source of great energy and vitality.

When the settlement began in the mid 1930s, it was beyond the city limits. It was a swampy dumping ground for garbage and unwanted squatters from the pavements of the great city. Now there are about half a million people living there.

Dharavi is like a huge refugee camp. The crooked maze of passages separating the tin huts are so close together that only the narrowest slivers of sunlight reach the earth. Some of the buildings are made of brick with tiled floors, but most are of rusting frayed tin. Roofs are covered with hessian, tarpaulin, polythene, anything that will help keep out the fierce heat of the sun in this barren, shadowless place.

The work of the women is the most visible. They sell tomatoes, aubergines or crimson onions. They cook on small fires at the edge of the channels of waste water, or they work at their sewing machines making garments for export.

The few open spaces in the slum are small mountains of waste— melon rind, banana skins, straw, paper, rags, cigarette packets, eggshells. The children work methodically through it all, collecting anything that can be recycled.

Cooking in Dharavi

 ▶Write down what you can 1 ▶ see 2 ▶ hear 3 ▶ smell and 4 ▶ feel.

▶Draw a picture of one of the scenes described here.

▶ Why do you think the author of this passage describes Dharavi as 'a source of great energy and vitality'?

▶ What do you think is meant by 'recycled'? (You will find some information on recycling in chapter 8)

Crumbling cities

In most Third World cities, it is the poor who suffer the worst consequences of air, land and water pollution. Yet, by taking lower paid jobs, recycling waste, making and repairing all sorts of goods, the poor perform essential services for the city. In many of the older cities of the industrialised world, where the infrastructure is now beginning to collapse, it is also the poor who suffer.

 ▶ Find out what problems older cities are facing today.

▶ What difficulties are shared by some inner-city areas in Britain and Third World cities?

▶ Imagine you are a young person in the early 1990s going to London to look for a job. You could face any of the following problems:

● You cannot get a job until you know where you are going to live.

● You cannot afford to pay rent because you have no money.

● You cannot claim Social Security because you have no permanent address.

● You cannot get a council flat because the waiting lists are too long.

● There are some empty houses. It is not illegal to stay there (squat) but the owner could take you to court and get you thrown out.

● You are cold, hungry, tired and dirty.

 ▶ Discuss in small groups how you would face these problems.

▶ Write a diary of your first week and how you are managing to survive.

Sleeping rough in London

Couple living in 'Cardboard City' on London's South Bank

 URBANISATION

Sprawling slums in Mexico City

The impact of cities

All cities use large quantities of *resources* and produce enormous amounts of waste (see chapter 8). The more cities grow, the more they affect the local environment. In industrialised countries, the main problem is pollution from traffic and industry. Also, surrounding land needed for agriculture is swallowed up by the spreading city.

Similar problems affect Third World cities. As many of the poorer citizens rely on wood for fuel, the trees in the surrounding countryside have to be cut down. This causes further problems because trees are needed to prevent the soil from eroding (see chapter 2).

Cities may affect the lives of people who live very far away from them. For example, the demands of cities for timber, or cheap meat for hamburgers, are helping destroy the rainforests needed by local people in tropical countries to make their living.

Sometimes land that was farmed for food is taken over by wealthy landowners to grow *cash crops* for people in the cities or for export. This pushes poorer farmers onto land that is not suitable for growing crops, so often they cannot make a living.

As more machinery is used on the fields, to produce more for the people who live in cities, fewer jobs are available for those who live on the land.

The more the impact of the cities is felt in the rural areas, the more people flock to the cities!

Push 'n' pull

When people migrate from rural areas to towns in the Third World, there are often factors that drive them from their home areas and others that attract them to the towns. In any particular place, some or all of the following may be true:

 ▶Make two column headings: PUSH FACTORS and PULL FACTORS. Put the factors below into the correct columns.

On the move in Botswana

- Rich landowners take over the land to grow cash crops, leaving the small farmers landless.
- There are sometimes jobs in factories or offices.
- Often only poor land is available for small farmers to grow food.
- There is more machinery, so fewer jobs on the land.
- People can make a living selling on the streets.
- People have to travel long distances to collect wood for fuel.
- Governments keep food prices low in the towns.
- Poor soils become eroded by wind or rain.
- Governments invest little money in agriculture.

 ▶How many of the PUSH FACTORS can be partly explained by the growth of the city?

▶Write down what you think governments should do to tackle some of these problems. What other benefits would come from these suggestions?

City of conflicts

Cuzco is a small city in Peru, in South America. It is a very beautiful place that attracts many tourists. It also attracts thousands of newcomers from the countryside who come in search of work. There is no room for the city to expand because it is surrounded by mountains. The government wants to build a new airport to attract more tourists. Without tourists there would be fewer jobs.

A group of squatters has just arrived on a piece of waste-land near the canal. They have built makeshift homes from scraps of plastic and cardboard. They are now threatened with *eviction* by the local council because the land belongs to someone else.

The local council is responsible for housing but receives very little money from the government, which has problems paying the *international debt*.

Now act out the role-play on the next two pages.

City limits

Some people believe that cities in the Third World will just go on growing. But there are signs that growth might be slowing down. Conditions may become so bad that cities can no longer function properly. Dealing with pollution, traffic congestion, securing food and energy, housing, refuse collection and jobs for all the people may become an impossible task. If that happens, cities may stop growing as they are no longer *sustainable*. Some people argue that the bigger cities are already becoming *unsustainable*.

The city of Cuzco

Group 1▶You left the countryside some time ago to find work in the town. You had a small amount of money so you were able to buy the rights to build on a piece of wasteland in the town. You were lucky enough to have friends to stay with, but conditions are very overcrowded and cramped. It is taking a long time for the legal building rights to be approved and meanwhile some other families have come and squatted on the land. You know that when squatters settle for a long time they are sometimes given services like water and electricity. Once they are settled, they will never go.

Group 2▶You are the new squatters. You have just arrived from the countryside. You have put waste materials to good use and built imaginative makeshift homes. Now you can go out and find work to pay for a better home somewhere else. Meanwhile you have nowhere else to go.

Group 3▶You are representatives from the government. You have come to Cuzco because you are interested in bringing in more money through tourism. Cuzco could attract more tourists, but it needs a new airport and at the moment there isn't enough land available. The wasteland is being sold off to newcomers from the countryside or used by squatters. You are also concerned that the squatters spoil the look of the city for the tourists.

Group 4▶You are the local council members. The law says you must evict the squatters. You want to listen to the arguments put forward by the different groups in order to make up your minds what to do.

Act out the council meeting where all the parties are present. Remember that the groups may not all agree among themselves. The council members will probably be divided, particularly between those who support the government and those who do not. They might consider the advantages and disadvantages of other solutions that have been chosen in the past. Here are some examples for you to think about and include in your arguments:

Harrassment One reaction by the authorities in many overcrowded cities has been to evict the poor from their settlements. One of the disadvantages is that the poor provide useful services that the city needs. And where would the evicted people go?

Providing services Another response has been to try to provide housing and services at relatively cheap rents. Who should pay for this? What about those who have no jobs and cannot afford even low-cost housing?

Self-help schemes Some authorities recognise illegal settlements and offer the settlers legal ownership of the land. They might provide roads, water and electricity once the settlements are big enough and well organised. This saves the cost of building new houses.

Chinese greengrocer in Hong Kong

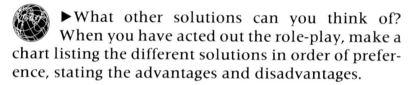 ▶**What other solutions can you think of? When you have acted out the role-play, make a chart listing the different solutions in order of preference, stating the advantages and disadvantages.**

The challenge facing all the world's cities is to become more sustainable—to provide for the needs of all their citizens rich or poor, while reducing pollution and other environmental problems. It's a big task—and the solutions touch on all the aspects of the global environment looked at in the following chapters.

 Look around your local or nearest town. Make a rough list of all the things you don't like about the environment. Now list the things which might be done to make things better. Discuss both lists with others, at home and at school.

Example:

Too much traffic   Encourage people to use public transport, ride bicycles or walk.

▶Take one example from your list. Plan how it could be carried out. Would it lead to other problems? If it seems a good idea, form a group to take it further.

Green cities

More cities are trying to 'go green'—to improve their local environments while having less effect on the wider environment.

Hong Kong, a very densely populated city of over 5 million people, manages to grow 45% of its fresh vegetables and produces 60% of its poultry. *Nutrients* from waste are recycled, local production means that less transport is needed, the green spaces make the city more pleasant to live in and the food is cheaper.

Many of Britain's larger cities have 'city farms', where people can grow their own food and learn about conservation.

Breaking ground ✳ soils

The Soil Story

If you had to think what all the people on the planet really needed in order to survive would you include the soil? You should, because life on Earth depends on the soil. All animal life depends on plants and, without soil, plants can't grow.

How much of the Earth's surface do you think is covered with soil? Have a guess. You'll find the answer by doing the following exercise with a partner or small group:

▶ Use a real apple to represent the Earth and cut it into four pieces. Three-quarters of the apple represents the oceans and one-quarter the land.

▶ Now take the quarter representing the land and cut it in half. One piece represents the land lived on by people. What proportion of the apple is left?

▶ Take the piece representing the land not lived on by people. Cut it into four. Three of these pieces represent the land that is too rocky, too wet, too cold, too steep or with soils too poor for agriculture. The remaining piece represents the land we can farm. What percentage of the whole apple is it?

▶ Now peel the skin off this last piece. This represents the fertile topsoil on which we all depend. It can vary in depth from about 2 m to a few centimetres.

Caring for the soils

Although the amount of soil on the planet is relatively small, if we take good care of it, it should last for ever. This is because it is a *renewable resource*. What do you think this means?

THE CHALLENGE

▶ HOW CAN WE MAKE BEST USE OF OUR SOILS WITHOUT DESTROYING THEM?

YOUR INVESTIGATION

▶ HOW DO SOILS SUPPORT LIFE ON EARTH?
▶ WHAT IS HAPPENING TO OUR SOILS AND WHY?
▶ HOW CAN WE PROTECT THEM?

Above: *soil erosion in Queensland, Australia*

Soil can be renewed in two ways. Firstly, the soil can replace naturally the *nutrients* that are removed through agriculture by breaking down fresh *organic* waste at the surface. Secondly, new soils are constantly forming through the weathering of rocks and minerals.

▶Can you think of any other examples of renewable resources? (You will find other chapters useful for this, particularly 4, 6 and 9.)

Soil that is not treated carefully is non-renewable. Just 2.5 cm of topsoil can take anything up to 2500 years to form, yet we can destroy it in under ten years.

For centuries, fertile lands have been turning into deserts, mainly through overuse and poor irrigation. Today many farmers are having to cultivate poor soils in order to feed their families. More trees are cut down for fuelwood (see chapter 6), more animals graze on fragile soil and more forests disappear to make way for agriculture. Eventually, the topsoil turns to dust and blows away in the wind or is carried away by the rains. This is called soil erosion. In the drier areas of the world, this leads to desertification.

▶Look at the map on this page. Name the countries where the risk of desertification is very high.

Map: Risk of desertification

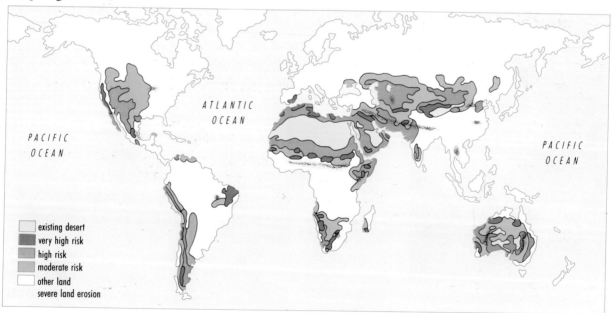

existing desert
very high risk
high risk
moderate risk
other land
severe land erosion

Warning—threat to the land?

If soil is a renewable resource, then why is more and more land becoming desert? Not all scientists agree about how far this is happening or what the reasons are. Often the farmers themselves, who may be causing some of the problems, have no choice but to farm the way they do. First, let us listen to what they have to say.

Let the farmers speak

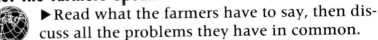
▶Read what the farmers have to say, then discuss all the problems they have in common.
▶Compile a list of the main reasons that farmers are destroying the soil.

Tomato harvesting in California

I am a tomato farmer in Northern California in the **United States***. I've been growing tomatoes on my land for twenty years. The only way I can pay my mortgage and labour costs is to get a full crop of tomatoes every year. And the only way I can do this is by using chemicals—more and more chemicals every year. I can't use cattle manure because all the steers are fattened in the Mid-West. I can't afford to go and fetch the stuff, though it's just what my land needs. Now nothing will grow here without chemical fertilisers—the soil is dead.*

I am a pastoralist *from* **Botswana** *in Africa. I used to be a nomad, travelling the desert with my animals and stopping to graze wherever there was vegetation. It was a good way of life, always on the move. Then we were told we had to settle and produce meat for export. We were given money by the World Bank to buy cows, and wells were sunk to provide water. Now the wells are running dry and becoming* salinated, *the soil is being damaged because we have to cut down all the trees for fuel, and keeping all the animals in one place is causing overgrazing. The soil isn't able to cope and is turning into desert. This development programme was thought up by 'experts' from the industrialised countries. No-one consulted us. Now look at the damage that has been done.*

Cattle farming in Botswana

I used to farm land in **North-east Brazil***, but my land was taken to grow sugar cane, which is turned into alcool, a petrol substitute for cars. Now I have moved into the rainforest in Amazonia to clear patches of land to grow food. But the soil underneath is very poor. It will only produce crops for one or two* *years and then I have to move on. I clear more forest and the same thing happens. After I leave, the cattle-ranchers move in and then after three or four years the land has turned to desert.*

My family has farmed the highlands in the **Yemen** *for generations. The slopes have been kept fertile by careful terracing that holds and slows the descent of the rainfall down the mountainside, providing irrigation and preventing erosion. Now the terraces are beginning to crumble as trees are cut down for fuelwood. Here we are becoming poorer and poorer so our young people leave the countryside to go and get jobs in the towns, and we don't have enough people left to look after the terraces. The government only gives help to farmers in the plains, where they can grow cash crops with chemicals and heavy machinery. We don't get enough help to keep our traditional way of farming going.*

I am a peasant farmer in **Senegal** *in Africa. I used to practice shifting cultivation. This means I would farm a piece of land for two or three years and then move on to give the land time to recover. The land has been taken over for settled agriculture and is now used to grow cash crops of peanuts to export to Europe to make into cooking oil. We were forced to move onto land which is very poor. If the rains don't come I'm afraid the soil I'm farming now will simply blow away in the wind and turn to desert.*

I am an arable farmer in East Anglia in **Britain**. *I grow wheat and barley. The government gave us loans to buy machinery and chemicals because they wanted us to produce very high yields from the land. I had to rip out the hedgerows so that the machines could move about more easily and so that every bit of land was used for cultivation. But the machines damaged the soil, and now the winds are blowing the topsoil into the sea. I use large quantities of chemical fertiliser to try to put some fertility back onto the land. But the soil is dead here, the food just grows in chemicals. What can I do? If I don't keep the yields high, I won't earn enough to pay my debts.*

Clearing rainforest in Amazonia, Brazil

Loading a spreader with chemical fertiliser in the UK

 ▶What are the main causes of damage to the soil in the six cases above?

▶Choose one case and suggest what could be done. Who would have to be involved in the changes?

SOILFACTS 2

▶About 44% of the arable soils of England and Wales are at risk from water and wind erosion.

Tractor harrowing, Hertfordshire

Pesticide poisoning

More than a million people worldwide are estimated to suffer from pesticide poisoning each year. About 20 000 of these people die.

Here today, gone tomorrow?

Over the last forty years modern, arable farming methods in Britain have enormously increased the yield of crops. This has kept us supplied with plenty of food at a reasonable cost. One of the consequences has been the damage that has been caused to the soil and the problems this will bring for farming in the future. Let's look at some of the ways that modern intensive farming can cause damage.

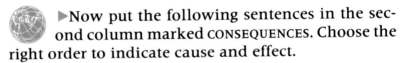 ▶Make two columns. In the first column, copy out the sentences below under the heading INTENSIVE FARMING TECHNIQUES.

● Land is cleared of trees and hedgerows to make room for more crops and machines.
● Machinery is used to plough the land and prepare it for crops.
● A single crop like wheat or barley is grown over and over again on the same piece of land.
● The seeds are sown in artificial fertilisers.
● Pests which attack the crops are controlled with chemicals called pesticides.
● Weeds which grow in the fields are killed with chemicals called herbicides.
● When the crops are harvested, nutrients are lost to the soil. They are replaced by artificial chemical fertilisers.
● The same piece of land is used over and over again without being allowed to lie fallow.

▶Now put the following sentences in the second column marked CONSEQUENCES. Choose the right order to indicate cause and effect.

● Without trees and hedgerows, the soil can be washed away by the rain or blown away by the wind.
● Herbicides kill the living things that create the humus (see column on page 15) and keep the soil fertile.
● If the land does not rest, the soil becomes exhausted.
● The essential nutrients taken out of the soil do not have time to build up again naturally.
● Machinery compacts and damages the soil's structure.
● Pesticides upset the balance of the soil and can be dangerous to people.
● Artificial fertilisers reduce the soil's natural fertility.

● Growing a single crop (monoculture) keeps on taking the same nutrients out of the soil and does not allow time for them to be replaced naturally.

▶Remembering what the farmers said, on pages 16–17, explain why you think these things are happening.

▶Suggest what changes you think can be made to protect the soils.

▶Many farmers are converting to less intensive farming methods. Try to find out about these changes. Should people be prepared to pay more for food grown in this way?

In some countries, particularly in the *Third World*, most of the best land is owned by a few powerful families. Often these families enjoy all the short-term benefits of modern farming techniques whilst the poor suffer the disadvantages. On the right is a story from a country in Central America called Guatemala.

Walking through the maize fields, Guatemala

▶Why did Rigoberta's family have to live on such poor soils?

▶Who or what do you think is responsible for the suffering of her family?

A child on the plantation

Rigoberta Menchu is from Guatemala. Her family had moved up to the highlands in the 1950s when the more fertile lands were taken over by wealthy landowners to grow cash crops. In order to survive, they had to work part of the year on the new plantations. This is what she remembers of her childhood:

'When I was about ten I worked on the cotton plantations, where it was very, very hot. We'd work long hours there for eight months of the year and in January we'd go back to the highlands to sow our crops. Where we lived we could barely grow maize and beans. The land wasn't fertile enough for anything else. The maize would soon run out and we'd be back into the overcrowded lorries to travel the long distance down to the plantations again.

Conditions on the plantation were very bad. When I was fourteen, my friend died of poisoning from the chemical sprays. I also saw one of my brothers die of hunger. We lived this harsh life for many years. Yet the landowner got richer and richer every year by selling the cotton abroad.'

	Wind erosion	Water erosion	Lack of natural fertiliser	Over-grazing	Loss of moisture	Loss of fuelwood
Tree planting						
Recycling						
Legume planting						
Herd reduction						
Bunding						
Terracing						
Agro-forestry						

Soil solutions

If the best land were shared more equally, the majority of peasant farmers would not need to put so much pressure on *marginal* land. This would require political changes. Meanwhile, there are some practical changes that will help the situation.

 ▶Look at the following list of solutions that have been applied in different parts of the Third World. Copy the grid on the left and tick the boxes to show which solution could help each problem.

● **Tree planting** Trees and shrubs planted in dry lands retain moisture in the soil and prevent erosion by wind. They also provide fuelwood.
● **Recycling** Crop, animal and human waste can be made into organic fertiliser.
● **Legume planting** Traditional vegetables such as beans and corn could be planted to restore fertility because they put nitrogen into the soil.
● **Herd reduction** Large numbers of livestock could be reduced to prevent overgrazing.
● **Bunding** In deserts, stones placed along contour lines trap moisture so shrubs and trees will grow.
● **Terracing** In hilly or mountainous areas traditional terracing ensures irrigation and prevents erosion by rain.
● **Agro-forestry** In some places, farmers have been able to combine trees, crops and animals in such a way that each helps the other.

 ▶What problems do you think farmers might face in carrying out these solutions?

Right: *terracing in the Yemen*

NEW LIFE FROM THE DUST

Over the last twenty years, many villages in the Sahel provinces of Burkina Faso in West Africa have lost a third, or sometimes up to a half, of their cultivable land through drought and *deforestation*. Trees have been burnt to clear land for agriculture or cut down for fuel, leaving the soil unprotected. In the dry season, winds blow the topsoil away and whatever is protected by the little plant life that survives is washed away when the rain comes.

Now the Burkina Faso government is campaigning to prevent bush fires, illegal tree-cutting and uncontrolled grazing of livestock. Most impressive of all is the way that local communities are finding new ways of conserving water to bring their land back to life. Building on traditional practices, they are constructing low barriers of stones, stalks and branches across their fields to stop the water from running away. Water is penetrating the hard ground, reducing erosion and increasing crop yields by up to 40–50%.

Now this simple method is spreading from village to village, with help from the government and aid agencies.

In some places, more recently, farmers have sown hedges and tree seedlings, dug compost heaps and built enclosures for goats. This is considered a more *sustainable* approach than using the stone lines on their own.

Bunding, Burkina Faso

 ▶Name all the solutions in the previous list that have been used in the case study above.
▶List those involved in bringing about the changes.
▶Why do you think the more recent approach (described in the final paragraph) is more sustainable?

 ▶Look out for examples of soil erosion locally – such as eroded footpaths. Can you do anything to reduce erosion and restore the path?

▶What about eating organic? Organic growing is kinder to the soil and organic food won't have been sprayed with chemicals. If you have a local wholefood shop, they will supply organic vegetables, pasta, rice, bread, etc.
▶Do a survey and find out what people in the street or at school think about organic food. Do they know what it is? Would they buy it? Do they think that, if everybody demanded it, it might become cheaper?

Water is Life

Did you know that 70% of your body is made up of water?

Without water, nothing on Earth could live or grow. Just as water runs through your body, it runs through the Earth, a network of veins and arteries providing life for plants, animals and people. Water is constantly in motion. It circulates from the oceans through evaporation to make clouds and then falls back on land as rain, flowing down rivers and streams towards the sea to repeat the cycle. The amount of water in the cycle is constant and cannot be changed.

 ▶ **Copy the diagram on this page and label it using the appropriate letters, as given below.**

A ▶ Many small streams join together to form a river.
B ▶ Rivers flow down to the sea.
C ▶ Some rain seeps into the ground, recharging underground water sources or *aquifers*.
D ▶ Some rain runs on the surface, forming streams.
E ▶ Rivers take water from high-rainfall areas to low-rainfall areas.

THE CHALLENGE

▶ **HOW CAN WE MAINTAIN A SUPPLY OF CLEAN WATER TO MEET EVERYONE'S NEEDS?**

YOUR INVESTIGATION

▶ **WHERE DOES WATER COME FROM?**
▶ **WHY IS WATER SO IMPORTANT?**
▶ **WHAT ARE THE MAJOR THREATS TO OUR WATER SUPPLY?**
▶ **HOW ARE PEOPLE OVERCOMING THESE PROBLEMS WORLDWIDE?**

Above: *impact of a drop of water*

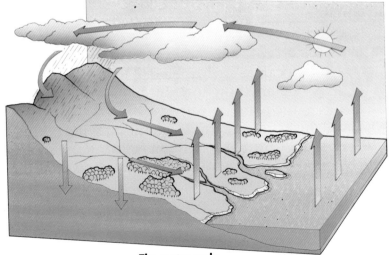

The water cycle

Water, water, everywhere

Two-thirds of the planet is covered in water. Of this, 97% is salty and found in the oceans. Of the 3% that is fresh, 79% is frozen in ice-caps and glaciers, 20% is under-ground (known as *groundwater*) and only 1% is found at the Earth's surface or in the atmosphere. Of this 1%, 38% is found in the soil, 52% in lakes, 1% in rivers, 1% in living things and 8% in the atmosphere, as water vapour.

▶ Draw three pie charts to represent 1▶ the world's water 2▶ where fresh water is found and 3▶ where surface water is found.

Although we live on a 'water planet', there are problems with supplying water to everybody. Some parts of the world receive much more rainfall than others and have a much more reliable supply of water, but in many drier areas present shortages are likely to become worse.

▶ Look at the map and name the parts of the world already affected by water scarcity. Which are likely to be affected in the future?

Clean drinking water and sanitation are crucial necessities. Yet everywhere surface waters are being polluted with untreated sewage and chemicals from industry and agriculture. Fifty thousand people die every day from diseases associated with dirty water. As with other key *resources*, we need to use water *sustainably* and reduce pollution. But how? Let's look at the problems.

Water warning!

All over the planet, the water cycle is being disturbed. Forests are being cut down, wilderness areas are being cleared for agriculture and rivers are diverted. These changes in the environment can have a big impact on water supply and can lead to water shortages, often in other areas.

But the greenhouse effect (see chapter 5) is likely to lead to lower rainfall in some places that now receive enough.

In some regions, underground supplies or aquifers are already being overdrawn or polluted. With growing population, more industry and the need for more food, world demand for water is likely to increase.

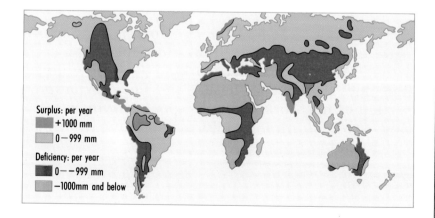

Global water

Surplus: per year
+1000 mm
0—999 mm

Deficiency: per year
0 — −999 mm
−1000mm and below

Household water consumption

(per person per day)

A ▶ With dishwashers, washing machines and sprinklers ▶ 1000 litres

B ▶ With a piped supply and taps ▶ 100–350 litres

C ▶ Using a public hydrant in the streets ▶ 20–70 litres

D ▶ Depending on a stream or handpump several miles away ▶ 2.5 litres.

Collecting water from a well, India

Where does all the water go?

Today there is as much water on the Earth as there was millions of years ago. But the numbers of people using the water and the ways in which it is used have changed dramatically. Like soil (see chapter 2), water is a *renewable* resource but, if it is used faster than it can be replaced naturally by the water cycle, there will be shortages. By the year 2000 we will by using ten times more water than in 1900. Where does it all go?

People use it

In Britain we tend to take water for granted. The average person living in a town or city consumes 100–350 litres of water per day for domestic use alone. Compare this with the 2.5 litres used by a rural dweller in the *Third World* who may have to walk miles to a stream to fetch it.

 ▶ Make a bar graph using the figures on domestic water consumption given on the left.
▶ Where in the world do you think you would find each of these households?
▶ List the different ways you use water in one day.
▶ What problems do you think you might face if you only used 2.5 litres of water per day for all your needs?

A day in the life

A typical woman in rural India spends 5 hours carrying water, 5 hours preparing and cooking food, 8–10 hours working on the farm (in season) and 4–5 hours collecting fuel and fodder (food for animals).

▶ Draw a 24-hour clock showing how many hours a woman in rural India spends on each activity. How long is her working day? How much time does she have for leisure and sleep? What proportion of her working day is spent carrying water? How do you think she could use that time if she had water nearby?

Irrigation channel for rice fields, near Timbuktu, Mali, Africa

Agriculture uses it

Domestic use is only 7% of the global use of water. Over recent years, irrigation for agriculture has increased dramatically, using 70% of the Earth's available water supply. Many irrigation methods are inefficient, wasting two-thirds of the water used, and can cause *water-logging*, *salinisation* or soil erosion (see chapter 2). In some countries large dams have been constructed.

 ▶ Read the story on the right. Draw a series of pictures to show what happened after the dam was built.
▶ Can you think of ways to irrigate the land that are less wasteful and do not harm the local villages?

Industry uses it

Water is vital to industry, which accounts for about a quarter of all water used. Although much of this water returns to the water cycle through rivers or the sea, the demand on water by industry is likely to increase.

 ▶ What might be the effect of a greater demand on water by industry? What other problems is the use of water by industry likely to produce?

Dam to drought

In India, over 1500 large dams have been built to provide irrigation (and energy for industry). This has meant that India could vastly increase the amount of wheat grown. But there can be problems with big schemes like this. Let's take a look at what happened to some Indian villages when a dam was built for irrigation.

The nearby river used to *recharge* the groundwater supplies so that wells serving the villages were kept full of water. When water was diverted from the river to feed a dam it could no longer recharge the groundwater supplies and the wells ran dry. Water had to be transported long distances from the dam.

The reservoir built to store the diverted water submerged large areas of forest, which meant less rain (see chapter 4). The river cannot recharge the reservoir as fast as the water is taken out, so diverting the river to make a dam has caused drought.

1 *Warning sign near watercress beds, Havant, Hampshire*

2 *Contaminated water source in Ethiopia*

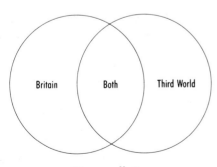
Water pollution

Pollution—something in the water

Did you know that the water you drink has been drunk several times before by other people? Our treatment system makes it possible for the water that is flushed away down toilets and drains to be treated and then pass into rivers, then through treatment works again before reappearing in our taps.

In the industrial world we take clean water for granted. This is not the case in poorer countries where many people take their water straight from the river. Many cities in Africa have no sewerage systems of any kind—most human excrement ends up in streams, gullies and ditches. In countries like Sudan, where water is scarce, buying water can take over half people's income.

In Britain, our water has become much cleaner since Victorian times, when diseases such as cholera were common. But over the last ten years new problems have arisen. Old sewerage systems can no longer cope, particularly with the large amounts of chemicals flowing in from domestic households, industry and agriculture. Eventually, polluted water reaches the sea (see chapter 9).

▶Look at picture 1▶and pick out from the items below the ones that tell you about water pollution in Britain. Then look at picture 2▶and pick out the ones that tell you about water pollution in the Third World. Some items apply to both.

▶Produce a Venn diagram (like the one on the left) to display your results. Write the headings on the diagram.

● **Sanitation** Many poor communities do not have sanitation and sewage treatment. Without these, supplies become contaminated and diseases spread.
● **Dangerous waste** Domestic households use soaps, detergents, bleaches, dyes, multi-coloured toilet paper, hair tints, unwanted medicines and cigarette ends, which all find their way into the water system.
● **Sewage** The sewerage system is under pressure and many sewers are falling into disrepair, some collapsing.

- **Acid rain** Burning *fossil fuels* (in cars and industry) releases sulphur and nitrogen gases which make *acid rain* (see chapter 7). In some areas this turns lakes and rivers acid.
- **Intensive farming** Agriculture uses large amounts of chemical fertiliser, which seeps into rivers and underground water supplies.
- **Diseases** Without access to clean water, many people catch waterborne diseases like typhoid, cholera, dysentery, diarrhoea and hepatitis.
- **Radio-active waste** Sewage treatment processes cannot cope with radio-active waste, which is sometimes dumped into rivers from atomic weapons factories and research centres.
- **Safe water** Well over half the people in the Third World have no source of safe water to drink.
- **Parasite diseases** Contact with water-related parasites causes diseases such as malaria, yellow fever, river blindness and hookworm.
- **Polluted oceans** In 1988 thousands of seals died in the North Sea and scientists said that pollution had weakened their resistance to disease. We eat great quantities of fish from the North Sea.
- **Toxic liquids** Britain discards 85% of rubbish into *landfill sites*. Toxic liquids can ooze out into the earth and contaminate the groundwater.

▶ Write two paragraphs to summarise the main differences between problems of water pollution in the Third World and Britain.

▶ Find out how many of your friends drink bottled water regularly. What reasons do they give? Do you agree with them?

A WELL WOMAN

Mwanaisha is a 23-year-old mother of six from a village in Kenya. She used to make seven journeys a day to a well to fetch water. In 1984, the Kenyan Water For Health Organisation (KWAHO) put in a handpump in Mwanaisha's village— and her life changed.

She no longer spends much of the day walking for water. The water is safe, and disease levels in the village have dropped. KWAHO is mostly run by women and fully involves women in the villages where it works.

Water pump in Kenya

Small dam, Sulawesi, Indonesia

High and dry

Some countries are tackling the problem of **water shortage** by building small dams for irrigation. These do not cause environmental damage in the way that larger ones can (see page 25). A possible solution for countries with coastlines is to make fresh water from sea water, but many poorer countries cannot afford the expensive desalinisation plants needed.

A less costly solution for water shortage is to use water more efficiently. In many Third World countries rows of stones placed on sloping ground (bunding—see page 20) are used to trap the rainfall. Tree planting is also used to improve groundwater supplies as well as prevent flooding and soil erosion (see chapter 4). Many industrialised countries *recycle* their water, using it more than once.

The simplest way of saving water, of course, is to use less. We are used to water being inexpensive but one idea to encourage water conservation is to increase the price.

 ▶If the price of water in Britain was raised, what effect would this have on consumers? Give examples of what might happen.

Safe not sorry

For many people in the Third World there is an urgent need for safe water. Here's what delegates to a United Nations conference said in 1977:

● Clean water and adequate sanitation are basic needs.
● The technologies required are relatively simple and readily available.
● The cost is very low.
● The results are quickly and clearly seen.

But four out of five deaths of people in the Third World are from diseases connected with dirty water. Providing water, toilets, drains and sewers for every household in the world would cost at least £500 per person. Who should pay?

Prevention is better than cure

It is much better (and cheaper) to prevent **water pollution** than to clean it up afterwards! Some industrialised countries are working to reduce the pollution produced by their industries, agriculture and sewage works, but most of these countries have at least some badly polluted rivers.

 ▶Here are some ideas for improving the water supply in Britain. Which should be introduced first?

● **Legislation** We need stricter laws to control pollution of our rivers by industry.
● **Fines** 'Polluter pays' means that farmers or industries should pay for any damage caused to water by their waste.
● **Incentives** Farmers should be given financial help to farm *organically* (see chapter 2). Industry should be

given similar incentives to produce *biodegradable* products and reduce the use of toxic chemicals.

● **Modernisation** Governments should modernise all sewerage systems.

● **Education** People need to be educated to understand how our water is polluted and what can be done about it. (They must understand that this may mean paying more.)

Water strategy

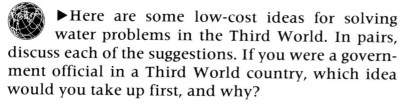 ▶Here are some low-cost ideas for solving water problems in the Third World. In pairs, discuss each of the suggestions. If you were a government official in a Third World country, which idea would you take up first, and why?

● **Water pumps** Simple, sturdy pumps to bring water up out of the ground could serve whole communities.

● **Sanitation** If there are pumps and a water system, then water supplies must be protected from contamination by sewage. On the right is one solution.

● **Community involvement** The local people must be consulted about what they want. They should not feel they are having something imposed from outside.

● **Health education** Health education would help people to understand the links between sanitation and disease and the dangers of contaminating water.

 ▶Design posters and slogans for an education campaign on water in your school. Ask if you could use the school assembly.

▶Find out from shops about water-efficient washing machines and other appliances.

▶With adult help, carry out a pollution survey of a local stream (see 'Resources').

▶What chemicals go into the water system in your house? (Find out what chemicals are in cleaners, bleaches, etc.) Do you use biodegradable products? Plan a campaign to persuade people to change their buying habits.

The VIP latrine—VIP stands for Ventilated Improved Privy. Pit latrines (in Britain we call them earth closets) are used worldwide. They are simple: sewage digests in them, they need no water and should not contaminate the ground.

The main problems are smells and insects, but the agency Wateraid has thought of solutions. A ventilating pipe (see right of picture) removes smells and a screen over the top stops insects getting in.

What's your water rate?

Try to discover how much water you use in one day. Here are some rough guides:

bath ▶ 75 litres
washing hair ▶ 20 litres
shower ▶ 15 litres
toilet flush ▶ 10 litres
washing up ▶ 7 litres
wash ▶ 5 litres
cleaning teeth ▶ 1 litre

4 Timber! trees

The Green Planet

If you looked down at the Earth from space, you would see that most of the Earth's surface, apart from the sea, is covered with green plants. Three quarters of these plants are to be found in the world's forests. Once a much larger proportion of the planet was covered with forests but, over the centuries, they have been cut down for timber, for farming and for mining. What do you use that is made of wood?

▶Go round the class each mentioning something you use in your everyday life that is made of wood. (Don't forget that paper comes from wood, too.)

▶Look at the photographs on these two pages and identify each one, using the following information.

- Tropical rainforests are rich and diverse.
- Tropical savannah consists of grasslands with scattered trees.
- Boreal forests have tall *coniferous* trees.
- Temperate forests are a mixture of evergreen and *deciduous* trees.

Life on Earth

Without trees and plant life, human and animal life on Earth would not be able to survive.

Look at the information below and make a list of the ways in which green plants, especially forests, help create and maintain life on Earth.

Plants use energy from the sun, carbon dioxide and water to produce food in their leaves, and to give off oxygen. This process, called *photosynthesis*, makes it possible for animals and humans to feed and also to breathe. Whether we eat meat or vegetables, we can trace all food back through the *food chain* to plants.

THE CHALLENGE

▶HOW CAN WE MAKE SURE THERE ARE ENOUGH TREES FOR OUR PRESENT AND FUTURE NEEDS?

YOUR INVESTIGATION

▶IN WHAT WAYS DO TREES SUPPORT LIFE?

▶WHAT IS HAPPENING TO THE RAINFORESTS?

▶HOW CAN TREES BE HARVESTED IN A SUSTAINABLE WAY?

Above: *what type of forest is this?*

Plants depend on soil, and it is forests which protect fragile soils from being washed away by rain. Forests act like a sponge soaking up rainfall before releasing it slowly and steadily into rivers.

Forests are an important part of the *water cycle*. Water evaporating from trees creates clouds. Plants, and forests in particular, regulate the amount of carbon dioxide and water vapour in the air. In this way, forests play an important part in affecting climate and reducing the greenhouse effect (see chapter 5).

Forests are a source of wood, fuel, fibres, food, animal fodder and medicines, not only for the people who live in the forests but for people all over the world.

Tropical hardwoods, such as mahogany or rosewood, are popular because they are beautiful and hardwearing. They come from the rainforests.

▶Look on the right (the globes) to find out which types of forests are being destroyed. Use the map to help you find out in which parts of the world these forests are to be found.
▶Discuss how the destruction of forests would affect people on the planet.

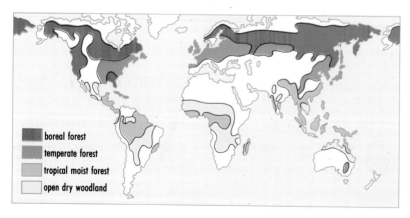

boreal forest
temperate forest
tropical moist forest
open dry woodland

World forests

Proportion of land covered by forest

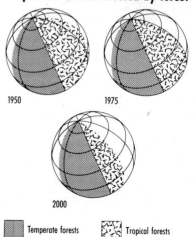

1950

1975

2000

Temperate forests   Tropical forests

Consumption of timber

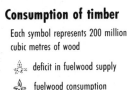

Each symbol represents 200 million cubic metres of wood

- deficit in fuelwood supply
- fuelwood consumption
- industrial consumption

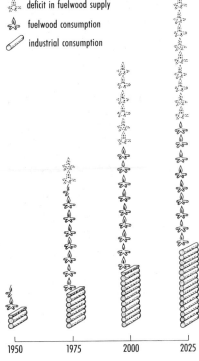

| 1950 | 1975 | 2000 | 2025 |

FORESTFACTS 1

▶Tropical forests contain more different types of plant and animal life than any other environment on Earth, more than half of all the world's species.

▶About one-third of the Earth's plant and animal species may become extinct by the year 2025. The loss of tropical forest is the major cause.

▶In harvesting tropical hardwood trees, such as rosewood and mahogany, up to two-thirds of the forest around them is destroyed.

▶An area of rainforest equivalent to 1.5 times the size of England is cut or burnt down each year.

▶All indigenous forest peoples are under threat from tropical forest destruction.

Losing the forests?

▶Look at the illustration on the left showing the consumption of timber since 1950. What is the situation in 2025 likely to be? What effect will this have on 1▶the forests and 2▶people?

Millions of people in the *Third World* rely on fuelwood for cooking and warmth, but trees are not only cut down for timber and fuel. Forests are often destroyed by fire to make way for agriculture, cattle-ranching, mining or hydroelectric schemes.

How does it happen?

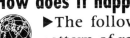▶The following sentences describe a typical pattern of rainforest destruction in Amazonia, South America. The sentences are in the wrong order. Copy them into your books in what you think is the most logical order.

● Cattle ranchers take over the land from the small farmers. The land supports cattle for another 3–5 years, then the ranchers move on.
● Roads open up the forest to groups of landless people who move in to burn the vegetation so they can grow crops to feed their families.
● The process of rainforest destruction is complete when the ranchers move on and the soil has turned to dust.
● The first stage is the arrival of logging companies who build roads into the forest for their machinery to cut and transport the trees.
● The land only supports crops for one or two years then the farmers move to another area of forest and start clearing the land again.

▶Trees absorb carbon dioxide. When they are burnt, they release carbon dioxide into the air. Look at chapter 5 to find out the effect.

Why does it happen?

In just a few years, rainforest that took 60 million years to evolve can turn to desert. Who is responsible?

▶Decide which of the opinions below belong to each of the following people. Match the numbers with the letters.

1▶A Latin American politician 2▶A spokesperson for a logging company 3▶A cattle rancher 4▶A peasant farmer 5▶A miner

A▶We're concerned about the destruction of the rainforest but we are in need of money to pay the *international debt* and to develop our country. The rainforests of Latin America are a wonderful natural resource which we must use. We can sell trees to the logging companies and ranchers can farm beef cattle for export.

B▶We used to have a plot of land on which we grew our food. Then a large company came along with permission from the government to throw us off our land. They needed it to grow soya beans for export, as this would make money for them and for the government. We had nowhere to go. We were desperate. Now the loggers have built roads into the forest we can move in again.

C▶I put my cattle on the land after the loggers and peasant farmers have finished with it. By then it's no good for anything else. We produce beef to make hamburgers for the United States. Our country needs the money.

D▶We used to farm this land, but now it has been taken over for mining by huge *transnational companies*. As we have no land of our own now, we are forced to work for them for almost nothing. We clear the land and convert the wood to charcoal to smelt the metals, such as copper, gold and iron. The companies then sell the metals to industrialised countries.

E▶It's my job to build roads into the forest so the machinery can get in to log the trees. Many major industries in the world depend on rainforest products and the demand is growing.

 ▶Write one sentence for each person, summarising their point of view.

▶Who do you think is most responsible for what happens to the rainforests?

▶How are we, in the industrialised countries, responsible? What could we do to help?

Surveying at an opencast iron mine at Carajas, Brazil

Cattle-ranching, North-East Brazil

The Chico Mendes story

Chico was a Brazilian rubber tapper who only learnt to read and write when he was eighteen. Soon after that, he became a trade unionist. He began to organise against the situation that the rubber estate owner fixed the price of rubber and the price of the products exchanged in return. 'When I learned to read, I discovered what kind of robbery it was and I began to organise so that people could sell through an independent trader.'

When the logging companies began to clear the forests in the 1970s, Chico's attention was turned from prices to land: 'For the first time ever we got together seventy men and women. We marched to the forest and joined hands to stop them from clearing.'

He was often arrested and beaten by the police for these activities, but nearly 3 million acres of land were saved.

Chico and other rubber tappers began to demand that they should be consulted about how the forests were developed. They wanted the areas used for extraction to be preserved. They wanted the knowledge of the local people to be considered. And they wanted a fairer distribution of the forest's resources.

His activities became known abroad and the importance of what he was doing was recognised worldwide. This brought him enemies among the landowners and 'developers'. Then, one day, as he stepped out of his own back door, two killers opened fire and shot him dead.

 ▶ **What was Chico Mendes trying to achieve?**
▶ **Why do you think he was killed?**

ROLEPLAY Imagine that the government of a rainforest country is facing demands for land from different groups. It decides to hold a meeting for all the interested parties.

From what you have read so far, decide who the different parties might be. Divide into groups representing each 'interest group' and the government, which will decide what to do on the merits of each case presented.

Brazilian rubber tapper

Once you have reached a decision, write a report of the meeting as if you were a journalist writing for a British newspaper.

Chico Mendes' widow, Ilzamar, shown outside their home, holding his portrait

What can we do?

We can support people like Chico Mendes by being careful about how we use wood in Britain.

 ▶ **How would the following help preserve the rainforests?**

● Use more softwood or local hardwood substitutes for tropical hardwood.
● Buy hardwoods from sustainably managed forests.
● Use wood more carefully, as a valuable resource.
● Reuse or recycle things made of wood instead of throwing them away.

Cut it out!

Is banning logging a solution?

In Thailand, South-east Asia, in 1988, flood waters carried mud and logs down the mountainside, and caused terrible damage to thousands of villages. The people protested so much that the Thai government had to ban all commercial logging. But the logging companies may increase their operations in neighbouring countries instead.

Illegal logging and clearing land for cultivation continues in Thailand, despite stricter controls which are also being adopted in other South-east Asian countries, where there is heavy forest loss.

▶ Why does illegal logging still take place?
▶ How do you think the land spoilt by logging could be used again?
▶ How do you think trees could be cut without destroying forests?

Medicinal compound

Sustainable forest management can prevent the loss of plants which could be a source of medicine, possibly providing cures for diseases such as AIDS. By ensuring a livelihood to the people of the forest, it also prevents their traditional knowledge of the medicinal uses of plants from dying out.

Before the industrial revolution in Britain, woodland industries existed which used every scrap of wood, timber, bark and foliage. The medicinal value of every plant was known.

Saving the forests

In order to preserve the forests of the Earth, we have to manage them in a *sustainable* way, without harming their ability to reproduce. Like soils and water, trees are a *renewable* resource, but only if they are used carefully.

Emilio Sanchoma is from the Amazon region of Peru where forest destruction is taking place. He is involved in a unique attempt to manage the forests sustainably.

 ▶Read what Emilio has to say, then describe in your own words what you think he is trying to achieve.

'I was born in the rainforest and have lived here all my life. Like all rainforest people, I know how to harvest the forest sustainably to feed myself, my family and my tribe. I grow crops like rice to sell and other crops and fruit to eat. I also keep poultry and other animals. We use the plants of the rainforest for medicines.

As rainforest people we are worried about our own way of life and about the future of the planet. We have been trying to find better ways of using the forest. In our area, the Palcazú Valley, the government has given us title to the land. We have set up the Yanesha Forestry Co-operative to log the forest on a sustainable basis.

We clear-cut a strip of rainforest 20–50 m wide, the same size as would be cleared if a large tree were blown down. It is wide enough to enable sunlight to penetrate the canopy and narrow enough for the plants to reseed themselves from the surrounding forest. Such narrow gaps don't affect the animals and preserve the forest soil against erosion.

The trees are felled with chainsaws and then taken out by oxen onto a main logging road where they are loaded onto the co-op truck. The oxen don't damage the soil and surrounding vegetation and are less expensive than heavy machinery.

We use every stick in the forest. Logs greater than 30 cm are sawn into lumber. Smaller logs between 5 and 30 cm are used for construction in our area. Smaller trees and odd-shaped scraps are made into charcoal and sold locally. We get 250 cubic metres of wood per hectare under this system compared with a typical logger's yield of 3–5 cubic metres.

Sustainable logging: the Yanesha Forestry Co-operative, Peru

FORESTFACTS 2

Using agro-forestry techniques, the Lacandon Maya people in Mexico produce 13 000 pounds of shelled corn and 10 000 pounds of root and vegetable crops per hectare per year. (Cattle ranches produce as little as 22 pounds of meat per hectare per year.)

Within a year of clearing the strip the forest has grown back above our heads. In 40 years we can come back and harvest it again.'

 ▶Draw a series of pictures to show how the Yanesha Forestry Co-operative logs the forest.
▶Why does Emilio describe this as sustainable harvesting?
▶What do you think people in Britain could do to help increase the number of such schemes?

Agro-forestry

 See if you can spot any tropical hardwoods in your school or home (they are usually dark woods). Check the desks, chairs, doors and window frames. Try to find out if alternative products are available.

Visit your local builders' merchant. See if you can spot mahogany, teak or rosewood. Find out where the timber comes from. Does the merchant know about the destruction of the rainforests? Would he or she use timber from a sustainable source if it were available? (See Friends of the Earth *Good Wood Guide* for more information.)

Plant a tree. Britain is the third largest importer of tropical hardwoods in the world. We have destroyed our own native forests and now take hardwoods from the tropical forests. In some places we have started planting native hardwoods again and recycling wood that has already been used. What ideas can you come up with for your area? Perhaps you could start a 'tree nursery' in the school grounds.

Green Audit (see also chapter 8). In your school, list all the different paper products you can find. Are any of them made from recycled paper? How could you use less paper? What about a campaign in the school to make others aware of the need to use less paper? You could carry out a survey and publish the results in the school magazine or on the notice board. Try making posters in your art lesson to let everyone know how important it is to save and recycle paper.

Using the wealth of the forests

The forestry co-operative in Peru is one example of sustainable development but it is not the only way.

In Kenya, the Chagga people have created a 'food forest' on the mountainside of Kilimanjaro. They grow fruit trees like papaya, guava and fifteen different types of banana trees used for food, animal *fodder* and beer. Below these trees are coffee bushes, while vegetables cover the ground. Cows, goats, pigs and chickens provide manure for fertiliser. All the plants are watered by irrigation channels which also contain fish. Growing crops and trees together is very successful and it is a form of farming which increases the production of the forest forever and also prevents soil erosion (see chapter 2). It is known as *agro-forestry*.

In the Amazon rainforest area of Brazil, there are people who collect non-timber forest products such as latex, resins and nuts, without felling trees. They collect and sell about 30 different products as well as food and medicines for their community. This is done on *extractive reserves*, which are areas of land which the rainforest people have demanded from the government.

The heat trap

If you've sat behind a window in a room, in a car, or in a garden greenhouse on a sunny day, you'll have noticed something about the temperature. It's warmer in than out. This is because the glass traps some of the warmth, stopping it from escaping. It's a useful effect—it helps the tomatoes in the greenhouse to ripen and it helps heat homes on sunny days in winter.

The same 'greenhouse effect' keeps the Earth from freezing. Without it, the average temperature of the planet would be 30°C colder than it is now. Greenhouse gases in the atmosphere act like the glass in a greenhouse and trap heat. This natural effect has kept the Earth warm enough to sustain life for hundreds of thousands of years. It is the only planet in the solar system to have such a protective 'blanket'.

▶ Wait for a sunny day. Place a thermometer in a sunny room or car, or a greenhouse if you have one, and another outside. Both should be in the shade. Measure the temperature every hour. At the end of the day, draw a graph to represent the results and explain them. Are other things, apart from the greenhouse effect, also influencing your results?

How the greenhouse effect works

Most of the sun's energy reaching the Earth's surface does so as light. About a third of this is reflected away by the clouds, the sea and the land. But some is absorbed, warming the air, sea and land. The land radiates heat energy back out into space. Some of this radiated energy—which we cannot see—is trapped by the greenhouse gases. As the level of greenhouse gases is increased, so is the amount of heat trapped in the atmosphere.

Now the greenhouse effect is working too well! Because of human activity, like burning *fossil fuels* and cutting

THE CHALLENGE

▶ HOW CAN WE SLOW DOWN THE GRADUAL WARMING OF THE EARTH'S ATMOSPHERE THAT APPEARS TO BE TAKING PLACE?

YOUR INVESTIGATION

▶ WHAT IS THE GREENHOUSE EFFECT?

▶ WHAT IS CAUSING IT?

▶ WHAT ARE THE LIKELY EFFECTS OF GLOBAL WARMING?

▶ WHAT CAN BE DONE TO FIGHT IT?

Above: *the sun, and the greenhouse effect, sustain life on Earth*

down forests, there is an increase in the amount of carbon dioxide in the atmosphere.

Since the late 1980s increasing numbers of scientists have said that the Earth is going to get warmer. Not all of them are in complete agreement, but most think that there are likely to be major changes in climate, with effects on all life on Earth.

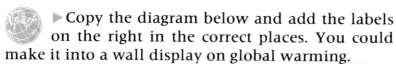 ▶Copy the diagram below and add the labels on the right in the correct places. You could make it into a wall display on global warming.

▶Write down as many things as you can think of that might be affected by global warming. Discuss your list with the rest of the class.

We all contribute in some way to global warming. That may sound worrying, but it also means that we can all help to do something about it. But first, we need to understand more about the greenhouse gases.

Warming up!
- Energy from the sun
- Some of the sun's energy is reflected back into space
- Some of the sun's energy is absorbed by the Earth and atmosphere
- Factories and power stations release carbon dioxide
- When forests are cut down they can no longer absorb carbon dioxide
- Burnt wood releases carbon dioxide
- Cars release carbon dioxide
- Heat trapped by carbon dioxide and other greenhouses gases
- Oceans warm, water evaporates and vapour adds to heat trap
- There is a limit to the rate at which carbon dioxide can be absorbed by the sea

The greenhouse effect

The carbon cycle

Do you know how *photosynthesis* works? (See chapter 4.) When carbon dioxide (CO_2) in the atmosphere is taken in by plants, the carbon is converted into living tissue and plant leaves. When plants die and decompose, or are burnt, the carbon in them combines with oxygen in the air to make carbon dioxide again.

Humans have upset this balance by burning fossilised plants in the form of coal or gas and clearing or burning forests. This way they have added to the amount of carbon dioxide in the atmosphere.

 ▶Compare the two graphs showing global production of carbon dioxide and global warming.
▶Why do you think there has been a rise in carbon dioxide from burning fossil fuels since 1860 (see chapters 1 and 6)?
▶How were fossil fuels originally formed? How does this explain why burning fossil fuels releases carbon dioxide?
▶Why does burning trees (see chapter 4) increase the amount of carbon dioxide in the atmosphere?

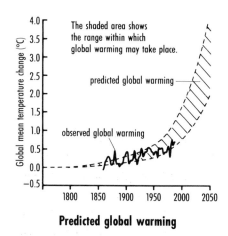

Annual global emissions of carbon (carbon dioxide equivalents) from fossil fuels since 1860

Predicted global warming

Other greenhouse gases

Is carbon dioxide the only gas that adds to the greenhouse effect? Water vapour is a key greenhouse gas too. It is increased as global warming causes more evaporation from the oceans. Other important greenhouse gases are:

● **Methane** This gas is produced when *organic* material breaks down or decomposes. It is given off from rice paddy fields, natural swamps, gas and oil wells, cows and other animals and also from *landfill sites* (see chapter 8).
● **Nitrous oxide** Given off from nitrogen based fertilisers used in agriculture, and from burning fossil fuels.
● **Chlorofluorocarbons (CFCs)** Man-made gases used as a coolant in fridges, for making foam packaging and foam-filled seats, and in some aerosols.
● **Ozone** Ozone in the lower atmosphere (not to be confused with ozone in the upper atmosphere) is a polluting gas resulting from car exhaust fumes reacting with sunlight.

▶What are the six greenhouse gases?

▶In groups of six, each of you choose one greenhouse gas and draw a picture to illustrate where it comes from. Label your picture with one of the sentences above. Add the pictures to your wall display.

▶Look at the table on the right. Draw a bar graph to represent the figures in the left-hand column.

▶Now look at the right-hand column. It shows how much more warming each molecule of the other gases produces than carbon dioxide. Which gas is likely to cause the most global warming if used in higher quantities?

▶For any one of these gases, try to find out what is being done to cut its production 1▶in this country and 2▶globally or in other countries. What sort of problems are involved? Write up your report for the display.

	Proportion of global warming caused (percentage)	Warming effect compared to carbon dioxide
Carbon dioxide	50	1×
Methane	18	30×
Nitrous oxide	12	200×
CFCs	14	10 000×
Ozone	6	150×

Signs of change

Ever since the late 1980s, there has been argument surrounding the greenhouse effect. It is difficult for scientists to be really certain that their theories are correct or to make firm predictions.

Some scientists believe there is evidence that the greenhouse effect is already changing our climate. For example, seven of the warmest ten years since records began were in the 1980s. Another example is the 'freak' weather patterns that have occurred worldwide over the last few years. The 'great storm' of October 1987 which swept across the South of England was one instance, and some people link the drought in much of Europe in 1990 with the greenhouse effect.

▶Find out about 'freak' weather conditions that have happened in this country and overseas. What views do people have about them? Do you think global warming has already started? Discuss your ideas with friends and family.

A gas-tly mistake?

When chlorofluorocarbons (CFCs) were produced to act as a coolant in fridges, scientists were pleased that the inventor, Thomas Midgley, had come up with what seemed like a safe, useful gas. It was only many years later that it was realised that CFCs not only help destroy the protective ozone layer in the upper atmosphere but also act as a powerful greenhouse gas. Now climate scientists are calling for the phasing out of all CFCs.

Stop waffling!

As long ago as 1896, a Swedish scientist predicted that if carbon dioxide levels increased, it would raise world temperatures. But most people only became aware of this effect in 1988 when newspapers around the world quoted a North American scientist, Jim Hansen, who said: 'It is time to stop waffling . . . and say that the evidence is pretty strong that the greenhouse effect is here.'

Floods in Bangladesh, 1988

A changing world

People have different ideas about the effects of global warming. Politicians in some countries are not too worried. They think that, with a warmer climate, farming might benefit. But many scientists predict huge disruptions to agriculture, affecting whole societies. This could lead to mass migration and disaster for many.

Evidence on the greenhouse effect has been reviewed by a group of over 300 scientists from 20 countries, the Intergovernmental Panel on Climatic Change (IPCC).

The IPCC predicted in 1990 that by the year 2020 the average global temperature would be 1.3°C higher, and that by 2070 it could be 3°C higher. This may not sound very much but a 3°C rise would make the world warmer than it has been for at least 120 000 years. The IPCC says that changes will not be even. Some regions, particularly in the *Third World*, will suffer more than others.

What could happen?

Although many uncertainties remain, the IPCC's *climate models* suggest that these changes could take place:

● **Climate** The warmer *climatic zones* will expand towards the poles, increasing temperatures globally.

● **Plant and animal life** Some species will not be able to adapt and will be lost.

● **The water cycle** (see chapter 3) There will be more rainfall in some areas and less in others.

● **Sea level** There could be changes of a metre or more. Warmed sea water will expand and cause flooding in low-lying areas. (The Nile Delta in Egypt, the Ganges Delta in India and Bangladesh and some islands in the Pacific are at risk. So, also, is the coastline of Holland and the East of England)

● **Agriculture** Southern Europe, the Mediterranean area, North Africa and North America are all likely to experience falls in production, while crops in northern Europe and northern Asia may grow better.

● **Trade** between countries will alter as a result of changes in agriculture. Some Third World countries will no longer be able to rely on the export of certain crops.

● **Migration** of millions of people from flood- and drought-stricken areas.

 ▶How many of these changes did you have in your list (page 39)?

▶How might changes in agriculture and trade affect our lives in Britain?

▶Look at the map on this page and, using an atlas, name the parts of the world that are most likely to be affected by flooding.

▶How do you think the worst effects of flooding could be prevented ?

▶What do you think might happen to the people who have to leave their homes or even their countries?

▶Why do you think the changes will be harder to cope with in the Third World than in the industrialised countries?

▶Draw a block graph to represent the figures on the right. What do the differences show? Which of these countries do you think should act first to reduce global warming?

Who is responsible?

Some countries produce more carbon dioxide than others. For example, the amount produced in North America is equivalent to 4.7 tonnes per person. In Western Europe it is 2.3 tonnes, in Africa 0.1 tonnes and in Latin America 0.1 tonnes.

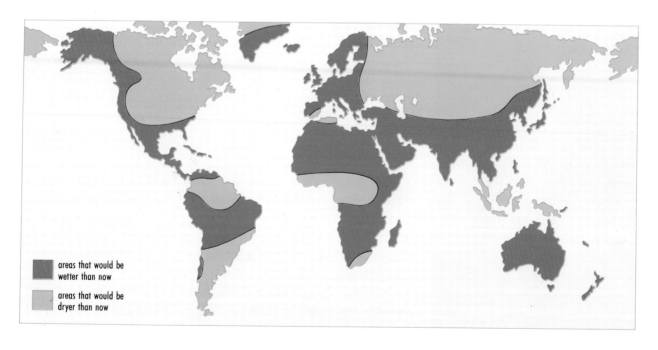

areas that would be wetter than now

areas that would be dryer than now

Effect of a doubling of carbon dioxide in the atmosphere

Action outside the 2nd World Climate Conference, Geneva, Switzerland—7 November 1990

A bright idea

In the United States there is a federal law that requires all electrical appliances to be energy efficient (see chapter 6). This should save as much electricity over the next ten years as would be produced by 21 power stations. Some power companies give away energy-efficient light bulbs—it's cheaper than building new power stations!

Energy-efficient light bulb (left) and the kind you're used to (right)

Time to change

Most scientists now agree that some global warming will take place because of the gases already in the atmosphere. The best we can do is prepare for the effects of warming and try to slow the process down.

This will require changes that will affect our lifestyle. Here are three things that would make a difference if carried out in every country:

1 ▶ Reduce wasteful use of energy through conservation
2 ▶ Make much more use of different sources of energy, particularly renewable ones (see chapter 6)
3 ▶ Reduce deforestation (see chapters 4 and 6) and plant huge numbers of new trees.

 ▶ Explain how each of these measures would help.
▶ In what ways would they affect our lifestyle?
▶ What are some of the difficulties in making this happen?

Planet or politics?

Although people are concerned about global warming, they may not like the changes that would help reduce it. This makes choices for politicians very difficult. For example, one way of reducing carbon dioxide would be to put a tax on fossil fuels. This could cause prices to rise on food, heating and transport, and could hit the poorest people most.

 ▶ Imagine you are an MP and you have received letters from people who are worried that the government is not doing enough. Write a letter explaining why you might agree and also the reasons why it is difficult to make quick changes.

Acting together—now

The IPCC says that global warming needs global solutions and that no country can tackle the problem alone. But, when countries have got together at world climate conferences, they have not all seen eye to eye. Countries that produce most of the world's fossil fuels, like the United States, the Soviet Union and Saudi Arabia, are reluctant to cut production of carbon dioxide. On the right is a summary of some of the positions taken.

The IPCC says that, as the United States and the Soviet Union between them are responsible for 40% of the world's carbon dioxide production, they should take the lead. It points out that some European countries have set targets for stabilising or even reducing their carbon dioxide levels. But global warming will affect everybody, so all countries must agree to take action. The world cannot afford a delay.

ROLEPLAY Discuss the problem as a role-play, with groups representing countries. Use all the information you have learnt in this chapter and any other material you may have found.

 If governments must act to tackle the greenhouse effect, individuals can help too. Here are some ideas for things you can do:
▶Keep informed. Keep an eye out for newspaper and television reports on the greenhouse effect. Note any changes in predictions. Cut them out and add them to your display.
▶Divide into groups to make action plans related to one or more of the following topics: trees; energy use; recycling; transport; shopping; CFCs; home; politics. Here are a few ideas to start you off:
● Ride a bicycle instead of taking a car ride.
● Switch off unnecessary lights.
● Don't buy unnecessary electrical appliances.
● Plant trees.
● Insulate your home.
Compare your plans. Which actions apply to more than one topic? Present your action plan to the class with reasons for what you are doing. Put it into practice!

Who goes first?
Netherlands
Some of our best agricultural land is below sea level, protected by sea defences. These defences are being raised and strengthened against a rise in sea level. We contribute less than 1% of the global production of carbon dioxide but we are very concerned about global warming and we will cut our production of carbon dioxide by the year 2000.

United States
We think the scientific evidence on global warming is still uncertain. Besides, the world needs more energy. We are also worried about taking action that could interfere with economic growth.

Many Third World countries
If we cut our use of fossil fuels this will hold us back in our development. We need help from the industrialised countries to find alternative technologies that do not rely on fossil fuels. It is not our fault that this problem exists. It should not be us that are made to pay. We have more immediate problems to solve and have to find the money to pay our *international debt*. Unless we receive help with this, we can do nothing about it.

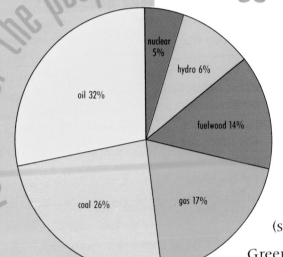

oil 32%

nuclear 5%

hydro 6%

fuelwood 14%

gas 17%

coal 26%

Source of energy—the sun

Without energy, nothing can be done or made—by people or nature. Our bodies need and use energy all the time, and so does the Earth. The Earth receives energy from the sun. Without the sun, the Earth would be a frozen planet. It is the sun which drives the cycles essential for life, such as the water cycle, the oxygen cycle and the carbon cycle (see chapters 3, 4 and 5).

Green plants take energy from the sun and use it to convert carbon dioxide and water to food in their leaves. As plants support all other living things on the planet, the sun is the source of energy for all living things.

SUN'S ENERGY → *converted by* → GREEN PLANTS → *eaten by* → ANIMALS → *eaten by* → HUMAN BEINGS

▶Looking at the food chain diagram above, explain how all living things on Earth get their energy from the sun.

For the whole of human history, until about 300 years ago, people got the energy they needed from *renewable* resources (see chapters 2 and 4). They burned wood for cooking, keeping warm and smelting metals. They used wind to drive windmills and water to turn water-wheels. Then coal came into general use, followed by oil and gas. These fuels are stored solar energy from plants, the product of *photosynthesis* millions of years in the past (see chapters 4 and 5). They are known as *fossil fuels*.

Fossil fuels made it possible for the people of Europe, North America and Australasia to build industrial societies. But this way of life needs large amounts of energy. The industrialised countries, with only one-fifth of the world's population, account for four-fifths of the world's energy use. Energy use is also a major cause of pollution.

THE CHALLENGE

▶HOW CAN WE ACHIEVE ENERGY SUPPLIES THAT ARE SAFE, CLEAN AND RENEWABLE?

YOUR INVESTIGATION

▶WHAT ARE THE PROBLEMS WITH PRESENT ENERGY SOURCES?
▶WHAT ARE THE ALTERNATIVES?
▶WHAT CHOICES DO WE NEED TO MAKE?

Above: *sources of world energy, 1987*

As fossil fuels took millions of years to build up, they cannot be replaced in a lifetime or even several lifetimes. This means they are a non-renewable resource and so will eventually run out. Although there is probably enough coal to last a few hundred more years, oil and gas could last only a few more decades.

▶ If you lived in Britain in the year 1600, what energy sources would you rely on? How would you use animals for energy?

Disappearing forests

For over 70% of the people in the *Third World*, the main source of energy is fuelwood. Another common source is dried animal dung. Fuel from plant or animal matter is known as *biomass* energy. Because it can constantly be replaced, it is a renewable resource—but only if used carefully.

More and more people in the Third World no longer have a reliable supply of fuel. For many families, the day begins with a long journey in search of firewood. People are having to cut down their future source of fuel in order to feed their children today.

▶ What happens if too many trees are cut down and not replaced (see chapter 4)?

▶ Write two sentences, one to explain what renewable energy is and one to explain what non-renewable energy is. What type of energy do we mainly rely on in the industrialised world? What type of energy do people in the Third World mainly rely on?

▶ Look at the photographs on this page. What do they show? Where do you think they were taken? Which are renewable sources of energy?

Switched on

In Britain, many of us take energy for granted. We can just turn on a switch or put a light to the gas. Yet a major question facing the world today is: how are we going to satisfy our demands for energy in the future? At present, about 75% of the world's energy needs are met by fossil fuels.

Dounreay nuclear power station, Caithness, Scotland

▶Look at the figures below and draw two pie charts to show sources of energy used by the industrialised countries and the Third World. Write a short paragraph to sum up the information given. What are the main differences? Which sources are fossil fuels?

Sources of energy	Industrial countries	Third World
Fuelwood	0.8%	43.7%
Natural gas	22.5%	6.0%
Hydroelectricity	6.0%	6.0%
Oil	39.1%	20.4%
Coal	27.1%	23.3%
Nuclear	4.5%	0.6%

The industrialised countries use far more energy per person than the Third World countries. In the future, as global population increases and Third World countries become more industrialised, the world will need even more energy. Just how much more depends on how efficiently we can supply and use energy.

Energy sources—pros and cons

In this century we have got used to inexpensive energy. But energy is no longer cheap, especially when costs to the environment are also taken into account. As each country plans its energy supply for the future, it has to consider the advantages and costs of each energy source.

▶Copy out the chart (top right of the next page) and fill in the boxes using the information given below. Try to find more information from other materials too. Which options are best for the environment?

ENERGY FACTS

▶In Britain, over 75% of our electricity comes from coal-fired power stations. The rest comes from nuclear and oil-fired stations, with only 1% from renewable sources of energy.

▶In the USA the Department of Energy has reckoned that the amount of available renewable energy in the country is 250 times its annual energy use.

▶The average person in North America uses about 330 times more energy than someone in Ethiopia, Africa.

- Using **fossil fuels** leads to air pollution (see chapter 7) and contributes to the greenhouse effect by producing carbon dioxide (see chapter 5). **Gas** is the cleanest fossil fuel, followed by oil, and then coal.
- There are enough **coal** reserves to last for at least the next 100 years, but **oil** may run out within a few decades.
- **Nuclear power** stations do not produce sulphur dioxide or nitrogen dioxide air pollution, and do not contribute to the greenhouse effect. However, nuclear power is very expensive, and produces dangerous radio-active waste that is difficult to store safely and lasts for thousands of years. This energy source uses uranium, which is non-renewable. The idea of nuclear power is unpopular with many people.
- Building dams for **hydroelectric power** often floods large areas of land, but creates no pollution. **Tidal power** (a form of hydroelectric power) can change estuaries and harm wildlife.
- The windmills that would be needed to generate **windpower** equal to what a power station produces would take up large areas of land, and be noisy. But windpower creates no pollution.
- **Solar power** is another possibility. Solar panels and solar electric cells are expensive, and less suitable for cloudy climates. They produce no pollution.

Energy source	Renewable?	Advantages	Cost to environment	Other problems?
Coal				
Oil				
Gas				
Nuclear power				
Hydro-electric				
Windpower				
Solar power				

Renewing our energy options

Renewable energy sources—wind, waves, sun, biomass, running water, and geothermal (heat from the Earth's crust)—are vast and could provide more energy than we would ever need. Also, they are *sustainable*.

But there are problems in capturing these energy sources in forms that are useful to us. What's more, we cannot just switch from fossil fuels to renewables, as much of our transport, machines and heating systems are adapted to using fossil fuels.

Some people say that renewable sources are uneconomic (though their costs are coming down). But as the price of fossil fuels rises (in money and in environmental terms), the world will come to rely much more on developing renewable energy sources.

Solar cells in use, South Luangwa National Park, Zambia, Africa

Electricity consumption in Dyfed

Category	kWh* million per year
Domestic	450
Agricultural	66
Commercial	163
Industrial	500
Total	1179

* kilowatt hours (units in which electricity is sold)

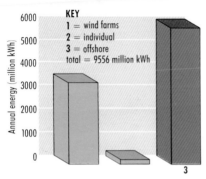

KEY
1 = wind farms
2 = individual
3 = offshore
total = 9556 million kWh

Wind energy potential

In the wind?

'Wind turbines are non-polluting and will help us save fossil fuels.'

'Wind farms can be very noisy and interfere with television.'

'I could install a small-scale wind turbine on my farm and use it for my own electricity.'

'It is windier in winter when most energy is needed, so windpower provides a good match with demand.'

'Windpower could increase the value of our land and attract industry to rural areas.'

'Wind doesn't blow all the time. Turbines will be used with other sources of energy.'

'I think hundreds of turbines in the fields will spoil the look of the countryside.'

Right: *wind farm, Carmarthen Bay, Dyfed*

The Dyfed Option

In Dyfed, in Wales, planners have been thinking about finding renewable alternatives to fossil fuels to meet demands for electricity. First, they needed to know how much was used. The table on the left shows current consumption of electricity in Dyfed.

 ▶Draw a bar graph to represent these figures. Give examples of how electricity is used for each category.

Renewable energy

The Dyfed planners decided to explore how they could generate electricity using renewable sources. They found:

● Solar energy (using energy from the sun itself) could help heat domestic and commercial buildings, but is not developed enough for generating electricity.
● Tidal power (using the rise and fall of the oceans each day) would involve building a *barrage*—not feasible.
● Windpower (using the wind to turn the sails of a windmill) came out as the most likely solution.

▶Look at the graph on the left showing the wind energy potential in Dyfed. Compare this to the graph you have drawn showing Dyfed's needs for electricity. Could Dyfed meet its electricity needs from wind farms?

▶Read, on the left, what different people in Dyfed think about wind farms. Make a list of all the advantages and disadvantages they mention.

▶Imagine you are a local resident. Decide what you think should be done and argue your case carefully.

▶What do you think? Should Dyfed go ahead?

Third World solutions

Two billion people in the Third World rely on wood as their main source of energy. Yet, as increasing numbers of people need to cook and keep warm, and more and more trees are cut down (see chapter 4), wood is becoming scarce. People in the Third World are growing more trees, and using fuelwood more efficiently (see right). They are also finding other sources of energy:

● **Biogas** is increasingly being used as a substitute for fuelwood. It is made by fermenting animal dung, human excrement or crop *residues* to produce a methane-rich gas. Although cheap to run, for some communities the biogas plants are quite expensive to install. Also, where the soil is poor, the dung may be needed as natural fertiliser.

● **Biomass fuel** Sugar cane, cassava and maize contain enough sugar or starch to produce *ethanol* when they are fermented. The ethanol provides fuel for vehicles to run on but has the disadvantage of using good agricultural land to 'grow fuel' instead of crops for food.

● Countries like China have built small-scale **hydropower** units to produce electricity. Poor communities need help with installation costs and training in technical skills to service them.

● Small, efficient **windmills** can be used for pumping water to villages more cheaply than diesel or bullock power. Local people need to be trained in building and maintenance.

▶ Summarise in your own words the different ways in which people in the Third World are trying to solve their energy problems.

▶ What are the main similarities and differences between the energy problems and solutions in the industrialised countries and in the Third World?

▶ Find out from other chapters in this book how we in the industrialised countries are contributing to the loss of fuelwood in the Third World. What do you think we can do to support the people whose lives depend on fuelwood?

▶ From the examples of Dyfed (on the previous page) and India (on the right), what do you think are the keys to solving the energy problems of the world?

Cooking on fuel-efficient stoves in Sri Lanka

Saving fuelwood in India

In rural areas of India women and children walk miles to collect a few sticks, while in urban areas fuelwood can take up to half a family's income. Let's look at some of the solutions being found by local communities.

As in other parts of the Third World, people have been experimenting with different kinds of stoves. The traditional three-stone open fire loses a great deal of heat. Specially designed stoves such as those shown above can save 70% of fuelwood used.

Some communities are getting together to plant woodlands not only for fuelwood but also for crops for food and fodder for animals. Planting trees has other benefits too (see chapters 2, 4 and 5).

Commercial plantations of fast-growing trees are being established, which yield up to 50 tonnes of wood per *hectare* per year.

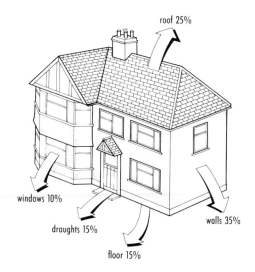

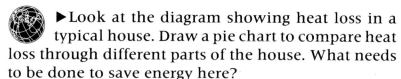

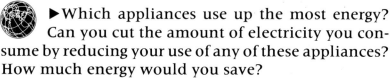

roof 25%

windows 10%

draughts 15%

floor 15%

walls 35%

Heat loss

Appliance science
Numbers of hours each appliance will run per unit of electricity

fridge freezer ▶ 12
light bulb ▶ 10
colour television ▶ 6–9
hair dryer ▶ 2
fan heater ▶ 1–2
steam iron ▶ 1
vacuum cleaner ▶ 1

Saving your energy!

Energy conservation is by far the quickest, cheapest and most effective way of making energy savings—and cutting pollution. Many energy experts believe that Britain and other industrialised countries could cut the amount of energy they use by half without affecting the standard of living or business and industry.

Local solutions

We can start in the home—and save on electricity and other fuel bills at the same time!

▶ Look at the diagram showing heat loss in a typical house. Draw a pie chart to compare heat loss through different parts of the house. What needs to be done to save energy here?

How often do you leave a light or television on when you leave a room? On the left is a list of common appliances and the amount of energy each uses.

▶ Which appliances use up the most energy? Can you cut the amount of electricity you consume by reducing your use of any of these appliances? How much energy would you save?
▶ Ask to see your electricity bill to find out the cost per unit. Then work out how much you spend on household appliances and how much money you could save.

National solutions

Some people say that, if energy prices were increased by the government, energy conservation measures would quickly follow. There might be more . . .
● Goods going by railway
● Commuters using public transport
● People living near their work
● Combined heat and power (CHP) schemes (see chapter 7)
● Energy-efficient products in the shops
● Recycling of materials (see chapter 8)
● Development of renewable sources of energy
● Insulation of houses and other buildings

▶Why would increased energy prices lead to more energy conservation?

▶How would each of these things help save energy? What else would save energy? What other advantages might there be? Any disadvantages?

▶If Britain took every possible step towards energy conservation, what might things be like by 2030? Draw a picture or write a story to show how you think it could be.

How quickly such measures are introduced largely depends on decisions by the government—some industrialised countries are well ahead of Britain in energy saving.

Global solutions

We have seen that local action can make changes to help solve our global energy problem. Worldwide, we need to develop more renewable resources to help meet energy demand, and offset the greenhouse effect (see chapter 5). In Third World countries, development of renewable energy sources will cut their dependence on oil and reduce debt (see chapter 10).

For the majority of the world's people, large-scale tree planting has to take place, which also counters the greenhouse effect. Some people recommend the expansion of nuclear power, but others say it carries too many risks. It is also too expensive for most people in the Third World.

Energy-efficient houses in Milton Keynes. Note the solar panels on the roofs.

 ▶Note down every time you think you could have done something to save energy (e.g. switch off a light, close a door, wear extra clothing indoors).

▶Check the buildings you use every day, such as your home or your school. Could any of these be done?

● Insulate the roof, walls, hot water cylinder and floors
● Double or triple glaze windows
● Draught-proof doors and windows
● Fit thermostats on individual radiators
● Use energy-efficient light-bulbs

▶Write to your local environmental group (like Friends of the Earth). Have they investigated energy-saving ideas for your area? If so, you could write and tell the council.

It takes your breath away!

Have you ever thought about what's in the air we breathe every day? The Earth's atmosphere is essential to all life but, in some places, the air is being poisoned by human activity. If you live in a city, the chances are that the air you are breathing contains harmful gases such as sulphur dioxide, nitrogen oxides and artificial ozone.

Air is made up mainly of nitrogen, with traces of other gases such as carbon dioxide, methane and ozone. Oxygen forms about 20%. All animals, including humans, depend on oxygen in the atmosphere. Oxygen is released by the green plants which cover the surface of the Earth. These plants also take in carbon dioxide, which animals cannot breathe, and the carbon is stored up as energy in the form of wood.

Air pollution results from our use of energy (see chapter 6). When wood and *fossil fuels* are burnt, they produce gases which contribute to the greenhouse effect (see chapter 5) and acid air pollution. Acid air pollutants harm people's health and also help cause acid rain that damages trees, crops, soil and buildings.

THE CHALLENGE

▶ HOW CAN WE REDUCE THE AMOUNT OF POLLUTION WE CREATE IN THE ATMOSPHERE?

YOUR INVESTIGATION

▶ WHY IS CLEAN AIR SO IMPORTANT?
▶ WHAT ARE THE MAJOR THREATS TO THE AIR WE BREATHE?
▶ WHAT IS ACID RAIN?

Above: *satellite map showing 'hole' in the ozone layer over Antarctica, October 1989*

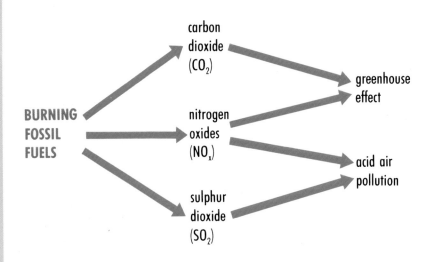

►Look at the photographs on this page and match them to the following statements.

● Acid pollution is damaging and destroying forests throughout Britain and Europe.

● In parts of Scandinavia and Britain, lakes and rivers are dying because of acidification and with them the plants and fish that live in them.

● Some buildings and monuments, such as Gloucester Cathedral, are being slowly destroyed as acid rain attacks the stone which gradually crumbles away.

AIRFACTS

►Two-thirds of the people who live in cities breathe air with high levels of sulphur dioxide which is putting their health at risk.

►In Sweden 18 000 lakes are so acidified that fish can't survive in them.

Taking a breather

High concentrations of sulphur dioxide from power stations or industry, nitrogen oxides from car exhausts and factories and ozone at ground level caused by car fumes can lead people to suffer from respiratory illnesses like asthma.

In many cities round the world, air pollution has reached serious levels. In January 1989, in Mexico City, it was so bad that school-children were given a whole month off school!

Acid air, acid rain

In the industrialised countries, such as Britain, we depend on oil, gas and electricity to run our factories, offices and homes. Most of the electricity is produced by coal-fired or oil-fired power stations. We also depend for transport on vehicles like cars and lorries, which are mainly run on petrol and diesel.

In Europe, the most serious damage caused by acid pollution is to the forests. In some countries, more than half the forests are dying. This is because the acidity in the atmosphere mixes with water droplets in the clouds and falls as acid rain, weakening the trees.

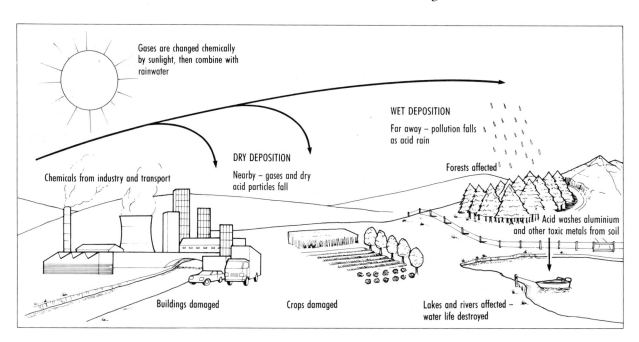

Gases are changed chemically by sunlight, then combine with rainwater

WET DEPOSITION
Far away – pollution falls as acid rain

DRY DEPOSITION
Nearby – gases and dry acid particles fall

Forests affected

Chemicals from industry and transport

Acid washes aluminium and other toxic metals from soil

Buildings damaged

Crops damaged

Lakes and rivers affected – water life destroyed

Acid rain

▶Look at the diagram and then copy the following five sentences into your books in the right order to explain the journey of acid rain.

● The clouds are often carried by the wind and the pollutants appear as acid rain in countries far away.
● When fossil fuels like coal and oil are burned, smoke and fumes containing sulphur dioxide and nitrogen oxides are released into the atmosphere.

- The rain falls onto the forests and causes damage, especially to coniferous trees.
- The pollutants in the air mix with water droplets in the clouds to form sulphuric and nitric acids.
- Acid rain also seeps through the soil into the *water table* and directly into Europe's lakes and rivers, killing fish and other water life.

Let the people speak

 ▶Read what three people in Europe have to say about acid rain and list the main things they are worried about.

'I live in Czechoslovakia. My family has worked here in the forest for at least five generations. Over the last ten years many people have been laid off work because the forests have been damaged by acid rain. I don't know what will happen to this area if the forest continues to decline. We all rely on the timber industry here. I worry that we might all lose our jobs.'

'I live in Sweden and we have been fighting to reduce sulphur dioxide and nitrogen oxide emissions for years. We have cut our energy consumption and cleaned up our power stations but well over half our acid pollution comes from other countries. A fifth of our lakes are damaged and many are already dead. Coniferous forests are suffering, which hurts our economy—and tourism.'

'I live in Germany. Not only are the forests dying but also the bird and animal species dependent on them. People's health is suffering through air pollution and through poisonous metals seeping into the drinking water.'

Who are the polluters?

 ▶Look at the table on the right and produce a bar graph to show which country produced the most sulphur dioxide (SO_2).

▶Now, with the help of an atlas, find out the population of each country. Which country produced the most sulphur dioxide per person?

▶Explain how everyone contributes to the acid rain problem. Why is international cooperation important if air pollution problems are to be tackled?

Oilfields ablaze

The Gulf War of 1991 produced massive air pollution when over 500 of Kuwait's oil wells were deliberately set on fire. No-one knows what the long term effects will be, as it may take years to put the fires out. Reduced sunlight and millions of tonnes of acid rain are likely to harm crop production and wildlife in the region.

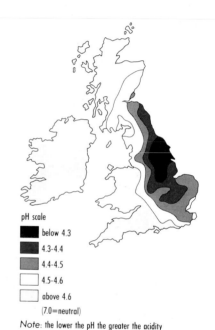

pH scale

- below 4.3
- 4.3-4.4
- 4.4-4.5
- 4.5-4.6
- above 4.6

(7.0=neutral)

Note: the lower the pH the greater the acidity

Acidity of rain, 1986

Country	Sulphur Dioxide Emissions (1988) (1000 tonnes per year)
Austria	62
Czechoslovakia	1400
Italy	1185
Netherlands	145
Norway	37
Poland	2090
Spain	1625
Sweden	110
Switzerland	37
UK	1890
USSR	5150

Death Valley—a success story?

Air pollution is not just a problem for the industrialised countries. Many industries are moving to the *Third World*, where environmental laws are less strict. In 1959 an oil refinery was set up in the valley of Cubatao, in Brazil. Other industries followed, and soon the new industrial town that grew up was nicknamed 'Death Valley' because of the pollution from the factories.

With help and encouragement from the local priest, the people of the valley organised themselves to protest to the government. They held demonstrations and attracted the attention of newspapers and television worldwide.

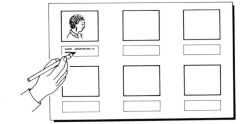

▶ Work in small groups. Imagine you are going to make a two-minute news item for *Newsround*, the BBC television programme for children. You have clips of interviews taken in Cubatao in the mid-1980s. You want to produce a story showing Cubatao then and now.

▶ Use a storyboard like the one on the left. This has small drawings of every scene. Who will you interview? What location shots will you show? What 'linking' shots will hold your news item together? Do you want studio shots of the presenter? Would you include any maps or pictures? How about some music?

▶ When you have planned your storyboard, write the script to go with it. You can include some of the following interview extracts. Add an update from your reporter on the spot (see *Getting results*, opposite).

Mother (Cubatao Victims Association): The factories here emit air pollutants several times a week. My daughter is like a thermometer measuring it—as the pollutants are released, she becomes ill. I have to take her to hospital two or three times a week to breathe medicated air.

Housewife: The companies here make huge profits at our expense. Most of them are controlled by foreign companies which come here because our government doesn't have strong laws about pollution. Progress shouldn't mean death as it does here. These people should accept responsibility for this disaster.

Protesters in Cubatao

Doctor: The hospitals can't cope with all the people being brought in with breathing problems: 30% of deaths in Cubatao are from respiratory diseases caused by pollution. The main cause of death is cancer of the lung, which also seems to have something to do with pollution.

Catholic priest: My work consists of getting people to come to meetings and explaining the health risks they are facing. I tell them that if they act together they can be more powerful and can bring about change locally.

Environmental consultant: Acid rain from the factories is killing the rainforest on the Atlantic coast. The soil is now so weak that the valley below is threatened with landslides. The vegetation is dying, fish are disappearing from the rivers and children are ill.

Getting results

The efforts of the people of Cubatao were not in vain. Some time later, in 1989, a reporter from *The Economist* wrote that the government had reacted to the worldwide attention of the press and television and put pressure on the factories to clean up. The report stated that the air was measurably cleaner now and that fish were returning to the rivers, after an absence of 30 years. Millions of seeds of pollution-resistant trees have been spread over the hillsides. The main industry still polluting this valley is the steelworks—owned by the government, which has been unable to pay for pollution control because of the *debt crisis* (see chapter 10).

Exhausted!

In 1985, the European Community ruled that all EC countries had to make lead-free petrol available (from 1989) and all new cars able to run on lead-free petrol (from 1990). This legislation came after a long campaign in Britain by CLEAR (Campaign for Lead Free Air). CLEAR argued that lead in the air damaged the brains of growing children. In Britain the government tried to increase the use of lead-free petrol by making it cheaper than ordinary petrol. Thousands of motorists are having their cars converted to lead-free.

From 1992, all new cars in the EC will have to be fitted with *catalytic converters* (see next page).

Above: *Lead-free petrol pump*
Left: *Cubatao, Brazil*

combined heat and power (CHP)

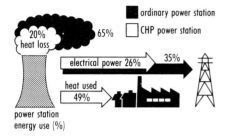

■ ordinary power station
□ CHP power station

20% heat loss

65%

35%

electrical power 26%

heat used 49%

power station energy use (%)

Drax Power Station, North Yorkshire

Liming an acid lake in Sweden

Cleaning up!

The ideal answer to the problems of pollution is to stop producing the pollutants in the first place. However, this is not practical in the short term, as we depend too much on energy from wood and fossil fuels.

What is possible is to use less energy through energy conservation. A lot of pollution could also be reduced by using different, renewable, sources of energy (see chapter 6) and by recycling more materials (see chapter 8). We can also take steps to clean up pollution at source.

 ▶Look at the solutions below for dealing with air pollution problems and make a chart showing the advantages and disadvantages of each.

Heating systems

Most power stations produce electricity with only 35% efficiency. A way to improve this is combined heat and power (CHP), which uses coal much more efficiently by sending the heat not used to power the station to homes, schools, factories, swimming pools etc. Fitting CHP is expensive, but efficient use of power stations is an important first step to take.

Removal of sulphur

Sulphur can be removed from coal and so reduce sulphur dioxide pollution. Desulphurisation is expensive and it produces other pollutants which have to be got rid of, usually in landfill sites (see chapter 8).

Catalytic converters

Road traffic produces 35% of nitrogen oxides. Catalytic converters can be easily fitted to vehicle exhausts to destroy the harmful gases produced by the engine. They are expensive and need to be regularly maintained.

Liming acid waters

Lakes and forests that have been damaged by acid rain can be sprayed with lime, which will help them recover for a while. However, in a short time they return to their damaged state and have to be limed again. It is expensive and only practical for some acid lakes. Liming can only tackle the symptoms and not the cause of the problem.

►Britain is the biggest producer of acid rain in Western Europe. What recommendations would you make about cleaning the atmosphere?

►Transport survey   Do a survey of transport used in your school.
● How many people come by car?
● How many people travel in each car?
● Could any of them use public transport?
● Could any of them walk or use a bicycle?
● Would any of them use public transport if available?

Write up your results and make some recommendations for the school to follow.

►Energy audit   Energy conservation is one of the most important ways we can reduce acid rain. Try to find out how much the school's energy bills are. For every unit of electricity used, 10 g of sulphur and 3 g of nitrogen oxides are released into the air. (Also created is 1 kg of carbon dioxide, the main greenhouse gas—see chapter 5.)
● How many ways can you suggest of cutting down the amount of electricity used?
● Is the school well insulated?
● What sort of light-bulbs are used? Could the school switch to energy-efficient bulbs?
● Is the heating used efficiently? Do the classrooms get too hot?

After you have done your audit, prepare a report with recommendations for changes. Remember you can cut electricity bills as well as reducing acid rain, so everyone should be pleased!

Smog over a Mexico City cement factory

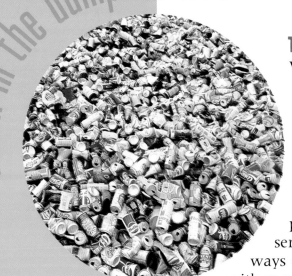

Too much rubbish!

What did you throw away today? Do you know where that bottle, paper, crisp packet or old pen will be taken? What will happen to it when it gets there?

If the Earth needed waste, like it needs the oceans, soils, rivers and trees, then we'd be doing pretty well. We are producing more now than ever before. The problems of waste are now becoming so serious that we all need to be thinking of ways of tackling them. The Earth can't cope with so much rubbish!

One of the problems is where to put it all—how to 'get rid' of the huge amounts we produce daily. Another problem is the fact that some waste is poisonous or toxic.

Thirdly, much of what we throw away takes a lot of energy to produce. Although energy shortages are not expected until well into the next century, energy *resources* are decreasing and energy use is causing pollution (see chapter 6). Reusing waste saves energy and materials.

What is waste?

▶ Some people say we live in a 'throwaway society'. What do you think this means?

▶ How would you define 'waste'?

▶ What is the difference between 'waste' and 'pollution'?

The average British dustbin is full of a lot more than just dust. It carries around 12 kg of household waste:

Paper ▶ 33%	Glass ▶ 10%
Plastics ▶ 7%	Vegetables and organic waste ▶ 20%
Textiles ▶ 4%	Dust and ash ▶ 10%
Metals ▶ 8%	Other ▶ 8%

 ▶ Draw a picture of a dustbin exactly 10 cm high. Using different colours, fill the dustbin in the correct proportions.

THE CHALLENGE

▶ HOW CAN WE CONSERVE RESOURCES AND REDUCE THE POLLUTION CAUSED THROUGH WASTE?

YOUR INVESTIGATION

▶ WHAT IS WASTE AND WHY HAS IT INCREASED?

▶ WHAT PROBLEMS ARE THERE IN WASTE DISPOSAL?

▶ WHAT IS RECYCLING?

Above: *cans for recycling, Leeds, West Yorkshire*

Buried treasure

Two children, who were staying with their grandmother, offered to dig her garden. In one corner they came across some old rubbish. 'Oh', said Gran, 'That's where my parents had their rubbish tip. There were no refuse collections in those days.' They carried on digging and were very surprised at what they found—pieces of broken plate, old coloured glass bottles, decaying leather boots, rotten wood and rusty metal hinges.

 ▶Why do you think the children were surprised?

▶If you had to bury your household rubbish, what items do you think would be included that your grandparents would never have seen?

▶How do you think the following facts have affected the problem of waste over the last two hundred years?

1 ▶The world's population has dramatically increased.
2 ▶The living standards of most people in the industrialised countries and some people in the *Third World* have increased.
3 ▶Science and technology have developed thousands of new substances and products.

 ▶Look at the following table. Find the towns, using an atlas. Draw a graph to represent the different figures.

Amount of waste produced in towns
(kg per person per day, 1982)

Industrialised countries

New York, USA	1.80
Hamburg, Germany	0.85

Third World countries

Medellin, Colombia	0.54
Calcutta, India	0.51
Cairo, Egypt	0.50

▶Why do you think countries with a low income produce less household waste?

▶How do you think Germany manages to produce so much less waste than the United States?

Landfill site, Rainham, Essex

A rotten experiment

What happens to things in a landfill site? To get some idea, try burying some materials in your garden (if you have one) or in the school grounds (if you can get permission). Dig a hole about 18 cm deep and put in some orange peel, a paper bag, some nails, a plastic bottle, and an unbroken glass jar. Put the earth back and mark the spot. Leave it for about six months. Then dig it up. What has happened to each material?

Out of sight, out of mind?

Burying rubbish in the back garden may have been a solution for our great-grandparents, but if we carry on burying our rubbish in dumps we may be creating a serious problem for future generations!

In 1990 it was estimated that 50 000 *hectares* of land in Britain may be contaminated with toxic waste, most of which comes from industry. In the United States, there are around 50 000 hazardous landfill sites.

Where does it all go?

'Waste disposal' is a misleading idea because rubbish can't just 'go away'. It has to be changed or treated in some way or else put somewhere.

For most industrialised countries, a convenient way of getting rid of waste has been to dump it into a *landfill site* — which usually means a big hole in the ground, perhaps left over after gravel has been extracted. About 90% of the domestic rubbish produced in Britain goes into landfill sites. Somewhere, one of these dumps is holding the rubbish you threw away last year. Do you know where it is?

 ▶Read the following, then make a list of some of the problems with landfill sites today.

Waste has to be collected and taken to the site. Some of London's waste is carried 80 km away by rail to Buckinghamshire and Bedfordshire. An important planning group has estimated that by the year 2000 all space available for household waste in the South-eastern counties in the UK will already be taken up.

The waste is buried under a thin layer of soil. When it rains, the materials in the landfill dump start reacting, and a toxic liquid can ooze out or *leach* from the site. This can contaminate *groundwater* supplies. Some new sites are lined to prevent this problem, but some old sites are still leaking.

As *organic* materials break down, a gas is given off. This gas consists of methane and carbon dioxide, which contribute to the greenhouse effect (see chapter 5). There is also some risk of explosion. Where chemicals have been dumped, there is a danger of toxic fumes being given off. If dumps are very old, no-one knows what is in them and how the chemicals will react. The cost of cleaning up old dumps is very high.

 ▶From looking at your list, suggest ways in which you think landfill sites could be improved. Who do you think should pay for this?
▶In Britain, there are a few schemes for drawing off methane gas and using it as a fuel. What are the advantages of doing this?

Warning

Detectable amounts of chemicals known to the State of California to cause cancer, birth defects, or other reproductive harm may be found in and around this area.

This warning is given to comply with California Health and Safety Code §25249.6 and does not constitute an admission or a waiver of any rights.

The industrialised countries produce almost all of the world's hazardous waste. In 1984, between 325 and 375 million tonnes were generated world-wide. Of this, only 5 million tonnes were produced in the Third World.

Safety or profit?

Each country is faced with the problem of what to do with its toxic waste. In some, like Britain, companies make money out of treating other countries' waste. Some environmentalists argue that this is a good thing because we have better disposal technology and can therefore do the job more safely. Others argue that Britain is risking pollution by treating the toxic waste of the rest of the world so that a few companies can make a profit.

As the environmental controls become stricter in the industrialised countries, some companies are tempted to ship their toxic waste to *Third World* countries. This is because they usually have poorer technology and less strict controls, which make treatment and storage cheaper, but also less safe. These countries are often pre-pared to accept the waste because they need the money they earn from it.

 ▶Do you think 'exporting' waste is a good idea? Give your reasons.
▶What do you think of the following alternatives?

1 ▶ Dumping waste at sea (see chapter 9)
2 ▶ Producing less waste in the first place
3 ▶ Treating waste in such a way that it can be used again

It's a waste!

Apart from the problems of waste disposal, throwing materials away is wasteful! Many of these resources are valuable and could be used again.

 ▶What do you think recycling means?

Charging the Earth

Did you know that making a battery uses 50 times as much energy as the power it provides during its life? And batteries contain polluting metals like mercury. In some countries, discarded batteries are collected separately from ordinary waste and re-cycled. In Britain there are very few battery recycling schemes, so it is better to use rechargeable batteries or mains power where possible.

Recycling—nature's way

Nature doesn't produce waste, or at least very little of it. You won't find nature's 'rubbish heap' anywhere on Earth, because nearly everything gets recycled. If it didn't, we wouldn't be here. The 'waste' from one organism is raw material for another. For example, humans and animals need the oxygen that is given off by plants.

As far as possible, we need to imitate the way nature has shown us. Some industries do this when they sell their waste products to other industries to make new products. But there has to be an industry willing to buy the waste. Also, it is only worthwhile if the cost of recycling is less than the cost of producing the original material.

 ►Describe other examples of nature's way of recycling.

►Find out if there are any industries in your area that buy waste products from other industries. Explain how this works.

Cities (see chapter 1) produce large amounts of waste, but recycling it is not always that easy to do in practice. The story on the left is about a recycling scheme in Cardiff.

 ►Why do you think the waste needs to be sorted?

►Why is it better for people to sort their own waste?

►Which of the materials do you think could be recycled?

Reuse refuse!

An increasing number of local authorities are trying not only to recycle but also to reuse waste. After suitable materials, like metal and glass, have been recycled, the remainder can be used in different ways. It can be:

● Pressed and dried and made into refuse-derived fuel (RDF). At present, Britain has few RDF facilities, but there are large plants in Europe and the United States.

● Made into compost and sold as an alternative to peat. In Britain there are very few facilities for this but, again, there are many in Europe and the United States.

● Burnt (incinerated). The energy produced from burning can be used for 'district heating' (heating houses and

A 'blue box' for recyclable rubbish

Cardiff is being launched as Britain's first 'Recycle City'. It aims to recycle 50% of its domestic waste. The campaigning organisation Friends of the Earth and British Telecom are providing assistance and money to get the scheme working. Industries, local government and the public are all being asked to cooperate.

Rubbish is collected from door to door and taken to twenty mini-recycling centres. Householders are asked to separate their waste into cans, plastic, glass, newspaper, and dry batteries. Special refuse vehicles with separate compartments for each type of waste make weekly collections. This is known as the 'blue box' system, and was first developed in North America.

factories) or to generate electricity. Incinerators have to burn at very high temperatures to make sure toxic gases are not given off. However, many of Britain's incinerators are too old to meet strict new European Community standards and may have to be refitted or shut down.

Although the domestic waste produced in Britain each year is equivalent to more than 6 million tonnes of coal, only about 8% is incinerated. Sweden burns 50% of its domestic waste.

 ▶Using the following figures, draw a bar graph showing the percentages of domestic waste taken to landfill sites in different countries. What could Britain do to reduce its percentage?

Britain ▶ 90% France ▶ 35% Belgium ▶ 35% Japan ▶ 30%
Denmark ▶ 30%   Italy ▶ 60%   Switzerland ▶ 20%

Byker incineration plant, Newcastle, Tyne and Wear

Why recycle?

Households in Britain throw out 4.5 million tonnes of paper and cardboard each year, but little of this is recycled. The government wants by the year 2000 half the waste from British dustbins to be recycled (from only 6% in 1990).

 ▶Look on the right and then draw your own diagram for recycling glass or metal.

There are some very good reasons for recycling. It . . .
● Reduces damage to the environment because less raw materials need to be extracted by mining, forestry, etc.
● Lessens the need for landfill sites and reduces pollution and litter.
● Saves energy and pollution in manufacturing.
● Saves costs on transporting waste and raw materials.
● Creates employment in recycling industries.

 ▶Why is it better to return a bottle and use it again than to crush it and make another bottle? Why do you think there are few returnable bottle schemes in Britain?

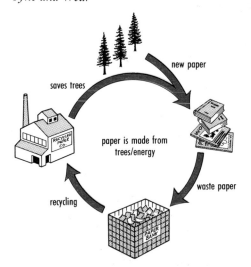

new paper

saves trees

paper is made from trees/energy

waste paper

recycling

The paper cycle

Overpackaging

Recycling tyres, to be used to make shoes and waterbags, Bobo-dioulasso, Burkina Faso

Oi! Packet in!

Have you ever wondered how much of the packaging in supermarkets is really necessary?

In 1990, a group of women decided to try to do something about overpackaging. Members of the group, called the Women's Environmental Network, took off all the layers of wrapping they thought unnecessary from supermarket goods, dumped the waste packaging in front of the supermarket managers and handed them letters explaining why!

 ▶ List any 'good' or 'bad' reasons for packaging that you can think of.

▶ Give three examples of products that you think come in too much packaging.

▶ Could a different package have done the job as well but resulted in less pollution and waste of resources?

▶ For one of your examples, design a package that requires few resources and could be recycled or reused.

Making it better

Because resources for industry cost more as they become scarce, industrialists have to use them more efficiently.

 ▶ **Imagine you are the managing director of a manufacturing company.** You decide what products the company makes. You are concerned about the environment and you want to reduce waste. You would also like to cut your costs. A report from some consultants suggests four options:

1 ▶ Produce less (reduce the level of production).

2 ▶ Design the products to last longer (make more durable goods).

3 ▶ Design the products so that they can be easily reused or recycled.

4 ▶ Recycle more factory waste.

▶ How would each help reduce waste?

▶ Which would be your first option and why?

▶ What are the problems or disadvantages?

▶ Is there a conflict between what's good for the environment and what's good for the company?

Recycling in the Third World

In many Third World countries, there is less waste per person than in the industrialised world (see page 63). Also, the kind of waste that is produced is different.

 ▶Look at the table and explain why you think these differences exist.

In Third World cities it is usually the poor people, often children, who collect waste by scavenging in rubbish tips (see chapter 1). Sometimes they work for the local government and sometimes for other people who sell what is collected for them. The work is unhealthy and badly paid. Sometimes it is the poor people themselves who recycle the waste in ingenious ways. In small workshops they use simple tools to make tyres into wastepaper bins or sandals, or turn tins into attractive lamps.

▶Many cities are trying to increase the amount of organic waste composted. Why is this easier in Third World cities than in the industrialised world?

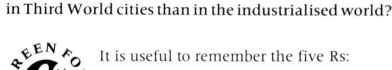

It is useful to remember the five Rs:

▶**Refuse** unnecessary goods and packaging. Try not to buy disposable things. Say no to plastic bags—take your own and use them again. Try to buy things in packages that can be re-used for something else.

▶**Return** materials when possible. Some shops will reuse your egg boxes or bags. Take things you no longer use, such as clothes or books, to a charity shop.

▶**Reuse** things (such as envelopes, paper, boxes, bags) wherever you can.

▶**Repair.** Anything that is repaired means saving resources and money!

▶**Recycle.** Take your paper, cans, bottles and plastic to your nearest recycling centre.

And, lastly, **remember** to do all this. Try setting up a recycling scheme at home or in your school. Why not design posters to put up around the school to remind people? You could even put one in your window at home.

Percentage by weight of urban waste (1982)

Material type	Brooklyn, New York	Lahore, Pakistan
Paper	35	4
Glass and ceramics	9	3
Metals	13	4
Plastics	10	2
Textiles	4	5
Vegetable and organic	22	49
Percentage of total waste that can be composted	26	73

Compost

If you have a garden, ask your family to save all your vegetable waste from the kitchen in a bucket with a lid. Save your garden waste, such as grass cuttings, too. Pile all the waste in layers in a spot in the garden and water it. Cover it with an old carpet. In a few weeks, you should have dark, crumbly compost for the garden.

If you are allowed to do this at school, experiment with different types of compost bin and insulation.

Think before you chuck!

Take a look at your waste bin. Can you think of a use for some of those things—the yoghurt pot, the plastic bottle, the cardboard box . . .

The planet Ocean!

If you were looking down on our planet from space, you might wonder why people call it Earth, as you can tell from the beautiful blue colour that most of the surface is covered by water. Perhaps Earth should be renamed the planet Ocean!

If you could pilot your own personal submarine, you would be able to explore this fascinating world, which scientists are only just beginning to understand.

▶Imagine this is a report you made of your underwater journey. Draw a picture to go with it, showing the shape of the sea bed and some of the life you found there.

'Diving down, I could see shoals of fish swimming near the surface of the water, then, as I glided towards the sea bed, I saw all different kinds of fish and seaweed. When I came to the end of the relatively shallow *continental shelf*, marking the beginning of the deep sea, there were some marvellous sights—huge underwater mountains higher than any on land, deep gorges and vast, flat plains, strange fish, and other creatures.'

How do the oceans support life on Earth?

▶Write a report on the different ways in which the oceans support life on earth. Make a list of five points from the following information:

The living world of the oceans is part of the Earth's *life support* system. All the plants and animals, from tiny microscopic plankton to mighty whales, are part of the interconnected *ecosystem* that has evolved over millions of years. The oceans control the Earth's climate patterns and affect the local weather of coastal regions and countries. The seas and atmosphere constantly interact through the exchange of gases, particularly water vapour leading to the formation of clouds. Four-fifths of the rain

Above: *where on the Earth's surface is this?*

comes from clouds that have been formed by evaporation from the ocean's surface. The sea absorbs carbon dioxide, which is one of the main gases contributing to the greenhouse effect (see chapter 5). About half the carbon dioxide produced by burning fossil fuels is absorbed into the sea. The sea is used by the people of the Earth for transport. It also provides them with food and serves as a dumping ground for their waste. Fishing and dumping have been going on for thousands of years.

Coral reef, Red Sea, Israel

Too big to be harmed?

In the past, people have thought that the seas were such vast and deep areas of water that they couldn't be harmed by human activity. Some people still think this is true. However, there are increasing signs that the health of the sea is suffering badly from pollution and too much fishing. There are limits to the amount of waste we can put into the sea and to the amount of fish and other things that we can take out. Scientists do not fully understand how the sea's ecosystem works and many are calling for caution.

 ▶Suggest reasons why overfishing and pollution occur.

Shoal of goatfish, Red Sea, Israel

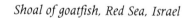

Goodbye to the herring

Fifty years ago the whole north-eastern sea-board of Britain lived and died by fishing for herring. Great fleets of herring boats pursued the shoals from Shetland to East Anglia, and the sailors' wives and families followed their journey on shore, gutting and barrelling the small, delicious fish. Then one day, the herring simply disappeared from the North Sea. Nobody knew why, but almost overnight a flourishing culture had vanished.

Fish 'n' ships—overfishing

 ▶Read the story on the left and suggest 1▶why the herring disappeared and 2▶what you think has happened to the people who used to make a livelihood from fishing.

So why does it happen?—a fishy tale

The cartoon on the left shows a few village neighbours who fish regularly in the local pond for food.

▶Describe what is happening in the pictures.
▶Decide what you think the men in each picture are saying to each other.
▶What could the fishermen do to make sure that stocks last and that they all get a fair share?
▶Which pictures do you think illustrate *sustainable* fishing and which unsustainable fishing?
▶Do similar problems of overuse occur with other natural resources, such as soils, water or air? (See chapters 2, 3 and 7.) What are the similarities?

Fishing need not necessarily lead to such problems. In many parts of the world, people use traditional fishing practices that do not endanger fish stocks (the total number of fish in the sea).

Natural breeding allows the stocks to recover after some have been taken through fishing. This shows that fish are a *renewable* resource. The problem arises when too many fish are taken from the sea.

The overfishing equation

Limited fish stocks + too much fishing = overfishing problem

Where demand for fish is limited and simple fishing techniques are used, fishing can take place on a sustainable basis. In recent years, though:

1▶World demand for fish and fishmeal (for feeding animals) has grown.
2▶Modern science and technology have improved the efficiency of fishing methods and enabled large-scale *commercial* fishing.

The result, in some areas, has been overfishing.

▶Match the causes and effects below:
Example: Navigation aids—Boats can go further

- Sonar radar

- Refrigeration

- Bigger boats

- Synthetic fibres for nets

- Mesh closes up tighter

- Can hold weight of big catches

- Boats can locate fish more easily

- Can catch small as well as big fish

- Boats can load bigger catches

- Boats can stay out fishing longer

All over the world, fishing is becoming a big industry, so there are economic reasons for overfishing.

 ▶Match the following in the same way:

Fishermen borrow money to buy larger boats

There is an *international market* for fish

Boats from different countries compete against each other

Encourages each to get to new fishing grounds first

They need to catch more fish to repay the loans

Encourages putting a lot of money into large-scale fishing for profit

 ▶Read the story of Pedro, on the right.
▶The government has given 'development' money for commercial fishing. What might Pedro think of this kind of 'development'?
▶To which other problems does Pedro refer, apart from overfishing? How are these problems linked?

Commercial fishing

The 'development' dilemma

In the Philippines, fish forms over half the protein diet of the average family. Sixty-three per cent of the fish are caught locally. Pedro is a fisherman from the island of Mindanao and here he tells us what is happening:

'I have a small canoe and catch fish close to shore. Over recent years, it has become much harder to make a living and feed my family. The government has given money to commercial fishermen using new technology, who have taken much of our fish. The fish are also being harmed by pollution from mining waste, industrial waste and sewage. I have heard that this is happening in many other countries like ours.'

Fishing in the Philippines

Time that solid waste remains in the sea

Bus ticket	2–4 weeks
Cotton material	1–5 months
Rope	3–14 months
Wool sock	1 year
Painted piece of wood	13 years
Tin can	100 years
Aluminium can	200–300 years
Plastic bottle	450 years
Glass bottle	undetermined

Sea pollution—a drop in the ocean?

'Everything goes somewhere' is one of the laws of the environment. With the waste products of modern industrial society, that 'somewhere' is often the sea. There is nothing new about this. People have been using the sea as a dustbin for a very long time and some argue that it can cope with pollution indefinitely. Some waste is dissolved or diluted so that it is not harmful. *Organic* waste can be broken down through natural biological processes (*biodegraded*). Nobody really knows if there is a limit to the amount of waste the sea can deal with, but the amount and variety has increased over the last few decades.

 ▶Do you think we need to take urgent action about waste in the sea? Explain your answer.

▶From what you read in chapters 3, 7 and 8, list some of the kinds of waste and pollution that could harm the sea.

▶Look at the picture below. Copy it, adding the following labels in the appropriate places:

RIVERS · PIPELINES · INCINERATION SHIPS · DIRECT DUMPING · ACCIDENTAL SPILLS OR DUMPING · ATMOSPHERE

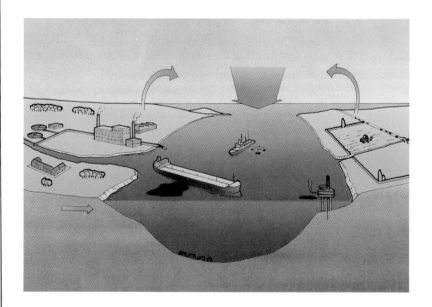

Sources of sea pollution

▶Use the following information to draw a pie chart illustrating where different kinds of sea pollution come from, worldwide:

Pollution from farming, industry and sewage ▶ 44%
Air pollution, acid rain and engines ▶ 33%
Maritime transport and fishing ▶ 12%
Dumping sewage and industrial waste ▶ 10%
Offshore oil production ▶ 1%

Living on the edge
What do the following have in common?

FISHING · TOURISM · SHIPPING · DUMPING WASTE AND SEWAGE · TAKING OIL AND OTHER MINERALS FROM THE SEA BED · SWIMMING AND HOLIDAYMAKING · BUILDING NEW MARINAS AND HOTELS

Answer: All take place on or near coastal waters, where most marine life is concentrated. All can result in pollution and destruction of natural areas.

 ▶Which of these activities do you think is most damaging to sea life? Give reasons for your answer.
▶For extra research, try to find evidence in support of your answer.
▶Discuss how these activities could be controlled.
▶To what extent do you think our lifestyle is responsible for the problems?

The challenge
As the world's population grows, there is likely to be more demand for fish and minerals, and more pressure on the seas. Unlimited fishing and pollution affect individuals, communities and countries. Protecting the seas is a major global challenge which we must all face. This means making decisions that are not always easy—decisions as individuals in our daily lives, as countries and as a world community.

Marina at Port Solent, Portsmouth, Hampshire

Clean-up operation after Exxon Valdez *oil spill, Alaska, 1989*

Oil on troubled waters
In March 1989, the tanker *Exxon Valdez* set out from Alaska, bound for California with a cargo of crude oil. The next day, the ship lay grounded on rocks and vast quantities of oil spilled into the sea. The accident affected over 1000 miles of coastline, damaging the marine ecosystem so seriously that some scientists think it may never fully recover.

During the Gulf War of 1991, several million barrels of oil were deliberately spilled into the Gulf waters. The oil caused severe damage to wildlife, endangered water supplies for coastal communities, and for many people, threatened a way of life dependent on fishing.

Just after the Gulf War, the oil tanker *Haven* sank off Genoa, Italy, its leaking cargo posing great danger to the nearby coastline and the Mediterranean sea.

What about fish farming?

Fish and shellfish farming, or aquaculture, looks like a promising way to increase fish yields. Fish are kept within a restricted area so they can be farmed sustainably. Just like farm animals, they are fed regularly, allowed to breed, and caught when there are plenty of them. Aquaculture has long been practised efficiently on a small scale by many societies, particularly in South-east Asia.

The FAO (Food and Agriculture Organisation) wants to increase the amount of fish produced by introducing large-scale fish farming. However, this can threaten the livelihood of local fishing communities and often leads to problems of widespread disease among the fish.

Fish farm, Scotland

Protecting the seas

Let's look at some of the solutions that have been suggested. How useful are they? Who would be responsible for putting them into practice? What new problems might have to be faced?

Tackling overfishing

Here are some examples of measures that have been taken in the North Sea to prevent overfishing of cod:
- A limit has been set to the size of fish that can be caught (smaller fish are left to breed)
- A limit has been set to the size of mesh that can be used (to allow smaller fish through)
- A quota has been set limiting the amount of fish that fishermen can catch.

Other options have been suggested:

Catch different kinds of fish · Eat less fish · Fish in someone else's territory · Import more fish · Use smaller boats · Leave areas of the sea alone until they recover · Increase the price of fish · Set fishing seasons · Limit pollution to allow better breeding conditions

 ▶Write each of these options on a separate card. In small groups, discuss how useful you think they would be and what the problems are.

Whose sea is it anyway?

 ▶Look back at the cartoon on page 72. Imagine that, instead of neighbours fishing in a pond, they are neighbouring countries fishing in the sea. What problems could arise?

In 1976, there was nearly a 'war' between Britain and Iceland over who had the right to fish in Icelandic waters. To solve this kind of dispute, coastal countries have declared zones 200 miles around their coastlines where only they can fish. What they have not been able to agree on is who has a right to the seas outside these zones. Should it be a 'free-for-all' or should it be officially shared out? What about the countries that have no coastline or that can't afford expensive fishing fleets?

 ▶How could such problems be solved?

Getting together

In March 1990 the third North Sea Conference was held with representatives from the governments of countries bordering the North Sea.

Some European countries had already banned the pumping of untreated sewage and dumping of sewage sludge and industrial waste into the sea. The UK, which has been referred to as 'the dirty man of Europe', agreed to stop dumping industrial waste by 1993 and to halt the other practices by 1998.

The countries at the conference agreed that by 1995 they would reduce by half the levels of 37 important polluting chemicals. Environmental groups criticised the conference for not considering pollution from agricultural fertilisers and radio-active waste from nuclear power stations, and for the time lag in carrying out the measures.

Greenpeace action to prevent dumping of waste in the North Sea

 ▶Why do you think the British government wants more time before it bans dumping?
▶Is this kind of international conference a good idea?

ROLEPLAY Act out the next North Sea Conference in your classroom. Some of you are representatives of the British government, some from other European countries. Some of you are concerned environmentalists.

 Find out if there are any sources of sea pollution where you live. Are there any industries putting chemicals into local rivers? Can your water authority provide you with information about water pollution?
▶Arrange a visit to your local sewage works and find out how much treatment the sewage receives. Or visit local factories that pollute waterways, or used to do so. Find out about plans to reduce, recycle or treat waste.
▶Visit a beach or shore, if you live near one, and count the different types of litter you find. Can you tell or guess where it came from? What kind of hazards could the litter pose for wildlife? Have a litter-clearing party!
▶Find out what Greenpeace has done about the dumping of toxic waste at sea. What do you think of this kind of action?

Fishing for facts

Got time for a spot of fishing? Visit your local fishmonger or supermarket. Count the different types of fish and seafood that are stocked. Write down their names. Try to find out as much as you can about where they came from. Do they come from distant countries? Do they come from fish farms? Ask your fishmonger about any changes he or she has seen over the years in the types and quality of fish available.

 OCEANS

Making the future

What do you think the future will be like? In part your own future will be how you see it now and what you make it. Try this exercise:

▶ Draw a line half way across a page and label one end B (your birth) and the other end N (now). Fill in key events along the line that have happened to you, Britain or the world since you were born. Now extend the line downwards as shown in the diagram.

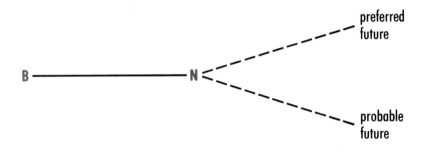

▶ Fill in what you think are likely events over the next 30 years. Label the line 'probable future'. Draw a second line upwards from N. Fill in the events you would like to see happen over the next 30 years. Label this line 'preferred future'. Discuss your time-lines with others.

▶ Draw a picture to show some aspect of your preferred future. Do you think this future is possible? Do you think the 'probable future' can be made more like your 'preferred future'?

What happens in the future depends on what we do today. For example, you might not get that new bike or pair of jeans if you don't save today; you won't get fresh vegetables from a garden unless you sow the seeds months earlier; you might not eat tomorrow if you don't go shopping today.

THE CHALLENGE

▶ HOW CAN WE FULFIL THE NEEDS OF THE WORLD'S POPULATION AND TREAT THE PLANET WELL?

YOUR INVESTIGATION

▶ HOW DO POPULATION GROWTH AND UNEQUAL SHARING OF THE EARTH'S RESOURCES AFFECT THE ENVIRONMENT?

▶ WHAT IS THE EFFECT OF TRADE AND DEBT?

▶ WHAT IS SUSTAINABLE DEVELOPMENT?

Above: if we support the Earth, it will support us!

▶Think of some choices you have made in the past which have affected your life today. What might have happened if you had made a different choice?

The quality of the environment in the future, and its ability to support us, depends on how everybody treats it today. As we've seen, the environment is under pressure across the globe. If we are to make a future world that can support or *sustain* people and wildlife well into the twenty-first century and beyond, we have to act now, and change many things.

First, we have to understand the problem.

A going concern?

Would you take a job like this? Unlike any other business, The Earth Co. Ltd is one we can't just shut down and start again somewhere else. We can't buy a new environment—we have to look after the one we've got. We all need to commit ourselves to the job of Planet Manager, whatever else we do.

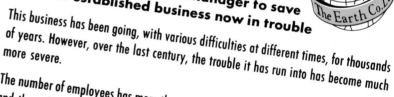

The Earth Co. Ltd
WANTED
Experienced Planet Manager to save well-established business now in trouble

This business has been going, with various difficulties at different times, for thousands of years. However, over the last century, the trouble it has run into has become much more severe.

The number of employees has more than tripled over the century (to 5.3 billion people) and they all want to benefit from the company's success. But some are taking more than their fair share of the wealth, leaving the growing majority to get poorer. The richer ones are lending money to the poorer ones and charging them *interest* on the loans. This means the poorer ones have no choice but to spend their lives trying to pay back the debt.

Meanwhile, the business is using up the raw materials and energy sources that it relies on, and these are becoming more expensive. It is also producing increasing waste and pollution, and spending vast amounts of money on weapons. If just a fraction of the money spent on weapons were spent on improving the people's living and working conditions, they could all exist in a decent environment. Many employees don't seem to understand that they all work for the same business, and they all depend on it having a lasting future.

 ▶If you applied for the job, what kind of changes might you want to make?

Supporting life

A successful Planet Manager would look after the natural systems that support life on Earth. These supply 'free services', including clean air and water, a climate suitable for life to exist, the formation of soils, the breaking down of waste and the recycling of nutrients.

These vital services are being harmed through human activity. It is partly a matter of human numbers and partly a matter of how we treat the environment and each other. We have touched on some of the main issues over the last nine chapters, but there are other important ones as well. These include:

- Health
- Food production
- Transport
- Arms and military spending
- Conservation of different environments.

 ▶ Choose any one of the above and investigate how it is related to the global environment. You can discuss your ideas in groups.

Before going on to see how we might manage the Earth and ourselves better, let's look at some of the other important things that affect the global environment and its ability to provide essential *life-support systems*.

Doubling times

Date	Estimated world population	Time for population to double
1650	500 million	
		200 years
1850	1000 million (1 billion)	
		? years
1930	2000 million (2 billion)	
		? years
1975	4000 million (4 billion)	
		? years
2020	8000 million (8 billion)	

In the Third World, children contribute to the family income

The numbers game—population

Once, a young man said he would work for his employer for only 1p in wages on the first day, as long as the wages doubled every day after that. His employer thought it was a good idea but soon became alarmed—the wage bill for the fifteenth day worked out at more than £160!

 ▶ Work out the wage bill for each day up to the twentieth day.

This story illustrates how quickly numbers can increase through doubling. The time it has taken for world population to double has decreased over the centuries.

 ▶ Copy the table on the left, then fill in the doubling times for world population.

►Look at the graph on the right and say where most of the population growth is taking place. Suggest why you think this might be.

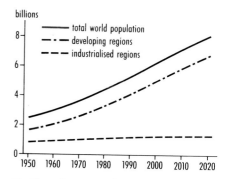

World population growth

In the industrialised world, the birth rate fell as people's standard of living improved. Now, the population in developed countries is growing less than 1% per year.

In the Third World, where most people are much poorer, families are usually large. More children die, so parents want to make sure that some survive. Children need to contribute to the family income and support parents in their old age. In many cultures people are proud of having lots of children. There are other issues. In Third World countries where living conditions and women's opportunities have improved, the birth rate has fallen.

 ►Why do you think better living conditions lead to a fall in the birth rate?

The needy and the greedy—sharing resources

The extremes of poverty and wealth found in the world are important causes of the destruction of the global environment. The growing population means more pressures, but it is not simply a question of numbers. The effect that any one person has on the world's environment depends on his or her use of its *resources*.

Middle-class couple walk past slum dwellings, Calcutta, India

The amount of resources that the world has is fixed and limited—it cannot be increased. But these resources are not shared equally.

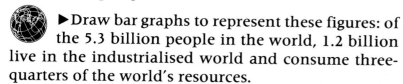 ►Draw bar graphs to represent these figures: of the 5.3 billion people in the world, 1.2 billion live in the industrialised world and consume three-quarters of the world's resources.

The rich minority also produces most of the world's pollution. The poorest rural people often find that they have to overgraze their land and cut forests to grow crops to feed themselves. Often they are forced onto poor land by governments who want the good land to be used for growing *cash crops*, to pay their debts to the richer countries.

 ►Why does an unequal sharing of resources harm the environment?

RESOURCEFACTS

►In the Third World, 1200 million people cannot afford basic shelter, clothing and food. Each year, 14 million children under five die from hunger and disease. These are big numbers, but they are made up of real people.

►The average person living in an industrialised country uses ten times more energy, fifteen times more paper and one-and-a-half times more food than the average person in the Third World.

Spraying coffee, a cash crop in Zimbabwe

For richer, for poorer—trade and debt

During *colonial* times European countries like Britain took *raw materials* from the countries they colonised in order to build up their industries at home. When the colonised countries became independent, large areas of land had already been transformed into huge plantations, which made them dependent on the export of these raw materials (such as cotton and tea in India).

Over centuries of trade, the prices paid for raw materials by industrialised countries has decreased in relation to the cost of manufactured goods bought by poorer countries, making the gap even wider.

 ▶Give some reasons why countries that produce raw materials are poorer than industrialised countries.

The debt crisis

As Third World countries became less able to pay for their manufactured goods with the money earned from raw materials, they began to borrow money so that they could develop their own industries or improve their exports. This led them into the *debt crisis*. To understand how it came about, try this exercise.

▶Work in groups of three. Each group has 30 strips of paper, each of which represents a large amount of money. Divide the strips so that one of you (A), who represents the rich nations and Western banks, has two-thirds of them. Another (B), who represents the Third World countries, has the remainder. The third in the group is the timekeeper, who gives the instructions.

▶The timekeeper should read each instruction and allow 30 seconds between each transaction. Payments are made on a regular basis, so the timekeeper must remind the other two when each 30 seconds is up. (It will be easier if this always takes place in the same order, such as A gives to B, then B gives to A.)

▶1 In the 1970s, Western banks and governments of industrialised countries lent money to Third World countries.

—**A gives 8 strips to B** (wait 30 secs)

▶2 The Western banks and governments charged regular interest payments on the loans.

—**B gives back 2 strips to A** (wait 30 secs)

▶3 The banks put interest rates up.

—**B gives 3 strips to A (instead of 2)** (wait 30 secs)

Commodity index as % of 1979-81 average prices

Debt in billion US dollars

Commodity prices and total Third World debt, 1970–1987

TRADEFACTS

▶A tractor which Tanzania could buy for 5 tonnes of its tea in 1973 cost double ten years later.

▶In 1987 alone the amount of manufactured goods that Africa could buy from the sale of raw materials dropped by 32%.

▶4 The Third World sold more raw materials to the industrialised countries to help pay back the interest.
—A gives 2 strips to B but
—B gives 3 strips to A (wait 30 secs)
▶5 In the 1980s the industrialised countries began to pay much less for the raw materials they bought.
—A gives 1 strip to B instead of 2
—B gives 3 strips to A
▶6 At the same time, the price of the manufactured goods and oil that the Third World needs has gone up.
—Add 2 more strips to those going from B to A
—B gives 5 strips to A
▶7 How are they shared out now?

What is happening?

Many Third World countries have found themselves with debt they cannot repay. This is a major cause of poverty and pressure on the environment.

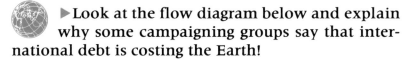 ▶Look at the flow diagram below and explain why some campaigning groups say that international debt is costing the Earth!

Many people across the world are calling for fairer trade between the industrialised countries and the Third World. They are also demanding that land and wealth is more fairly shared among people within countries.

▶Read again the sections on population, resources, trade and debt. Why would the ideas in the paragraph above help the environment?

Some environmental effects of debt on Third World countries

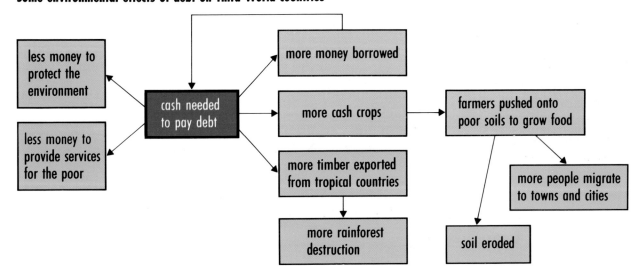

Making connections

As the debt crisis shows, many problems are connected. This exercise will help you work out some of the cause and effect relationships in this book. If you find it difficult, look again for clues in the book or from other materials.

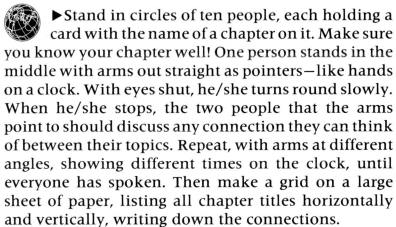 ▶Stand in circles of ten people, each holding a card with the name of a chapter on it. Make sure you know your chapter well! One person stands in the middle with arms out straight as pointers—like hands on a clock. With eyes shut, he/she turns round slowly. When he/she stops, the two people that the arms point to should discuss any connection they can think of between their topics. Repeat, with arms at different angles, showing different times on the clock, until everyone has spoken. Then make a grid on a large sheet of paper, listing all chapter titles horizontally and vertically, writing down the connections.

▶Alternatively, divide into ten teams and each discuss as much as you can remember about one of the chapters. Then draw a flow diagram (like that on the previous page), showing as many cause and effect connections as you can. When you have finished, put your flow diagrams side by side. How many of your ideas link up?

▶If you were able, what would you change on your flow diagrams to improve the situation? What effect might it have? Redraw the diagrams showing the changes.

These links show that things are very complicated, but also that a step in the right direction can help in all sorts of ways. For example, saving energy can reduce pollution, combat the greenhouse effect and save money!

Many people are realising that the problems have to be tackled together rather than in isolation, and that difficult choices often have to be made.

Polluted stream, next to market in Ujung Pandang, Indonesia

Children collecting waste on Smokey Mountain rubbish tip, Manila, Philippines

How to change the world!

How would you want to change the world? As we have seen, there are many challenges that have to be faced. The Earth is in trouble, but we have the opportunity to put things right if everybody acts now!

One of the most important ideas that has caught on in recent years is *sustainability* or sustainable development. You will have found these words in previous chapters. What do they mean?

Development usually means creating wealth (mainly through industry and agriculture) and providing services such as health, education, housing, roads, sanitation and other needs.

Sustainable development means providing for the needs of present generations without preventing future generations from developing too. This means only taking what we need and leaving the environment in at least as good a state as we found it. Instead of using valuable resources such as soil, trees and water faster than they can be replaced or recycled naturally, we must work with nature so as not to destroy the planet's *ecology*. We should save, rather than spend our environmental *'capital'*.

 ▶ Read the following and decide who is using their account sustainably:

Fred and Ann both have savings accounts of £20.00 at the Post Office. Fred spent the £2.00 interest he got in the first year and also £5.00 of the capital. In the next year he only got £1.50 interest. Ann is only spending the £2.00 interest a year that her capital earns.

Boy looking after young trees in forest development scheme, Gujarat, India

Left: *midwife giving a talk on family planning at a clinic in Burkina Faso, Africa*

We can't go on like this!

Putting sustainable development into practice is difficult. But more and more governments and ordinary people are realising that the sort of development we have now cannot last. We cannot continue to use up resources, produce large amounts of waste and pollution, keep most of the world's people in poverty, and harm the environment. This sort of 'development' will eventually make the environment unfit for human life.

Sustainable development requires a different way of developing and, for most of the world's richer people, it requires a change in their lifestyles. All over the world, groups and organisations and some governments are attempting to begin sustainable development projects. Some of these ideas have been described in this book.

▶ **From the previous chapters, list as many examples as you can remember of sustainable use of resources.**

What follows looks at some positive ways of achieving sustainable development both locally and globally. The Green for Go section on the last page will give you ideas of concrete things that can be done—by you—now!

Wood and charcoal stoves made from recycled materials, Kenya

Towards a sustainable world

The Worldwatch Institute is an environmental organisation based in Washington, USA. For some years it has been producing reports on what is needed to put the Earth on a sustainable course. These are the Institute's main conclusions:

Globally, the four key aims must be to . . .

1 ▶ Reduce pollution and slow global warming
2 ▶ Increase areas of forest to meet environmental and energy needs in the Third World countries
3 ▶ Increase food production
4 ▶ Slow down population growth.

These can be met through the following programmes . . .

Small-scale, sustainable fishing on the coast of The Gambia, Africa

A ▶ Large-scale tree planting
B ▶ More family planning advice and help
C ▶ Soil conservation programmes
D ▶ Increasing energy efficiency and conservation
E ▶ Developing renewable energy sources
F ▶ Protecting the number or diversity of plant and animal species
G ▶ Reducing or cancelling Third World debt.

 ▶ As far as you can tell, which programmes will help which aims? Match each aim number with one or more programme letters. Discuss your choice. Can you think of other ideas which would help?

The Worldwatch Institute says that this programme will cost a good deal of money—about £300 000 million (£300 billion) a year. It sounds a lot, but is only one-sixth of the world's combined military budget. How much is the military budget per year?

Farmer cultivating seedlings, Kenya

▶ The pie chart on the right represents a budget and programme which the Worldwatch Institute thinks the world should begin, in order to achieve sustainable development. If the total budget was $150 billion a year, how much would be spent on each programme activity shown?

If the world can afford this money, why isn't enough being spent? It all depends on decisions made by the world's politicians. For example, many politicians think that protecting their countries with military weapons is more important than preventing environmental destruction.

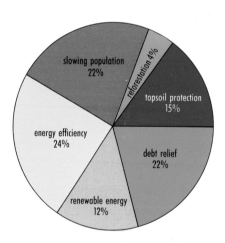

Budget for 10-year global sustainable development effort

▶ Which do you think is more important in the long run?
▶ How could you let your government know what you think?

The sustainability idea is growing, but it requires action and new thinking at every level, from personal to international, from local to global. Let's look at some more examples.

Working towards sustainability—UK

As we saw in chapter 1, cities have a major effect on the environment. Leicester, the tenth largest city in the UK, is attempting to 'go green'. It is Britain's first 'Environment City' under a new campaign which aims to make British cities more sustainable. Many groups in Leicester are cooperating to improve the city environment. They are focusing on eight main environmental areas—see the table.

Environmental area	Environmental idea/activity

1 ▶ Energy
2 ▶ Transport
3 ▶ Waste and pollution
4 ▶ Food and agriculture
5 ▶ Economy and work
6 ▶ Built environment
7 ▶ Natural environment
8 ▶ Social environment (the local community)

The following are a few of the environmental ideas and activities that the campaign aims to introduce or encourage:

a ▶ Advice to people about using 'green products'
b ▶ Using minimum packaging for goods
c ▶ Buying goods produced locally
d ▶ Having cycle parks outside employers' buildings
e ▶ Using returnable packaging and recycled paper
f ▶ Better energy conservation in buildings
g ▶ Protecting important wildlife sites
h ▶ Tree planting
i ▶ Wildlife areas at all schools
j ▶ Involving people in environmental improvements
k ▶ Education and information programmes
l ▶ Save energy campaign
m ▶ Sharing cars
n ▶ Clean up waterways
o ▶ City-wide recycling collections
p ▶ Discourage use of harmful pesticides
q ▶ Compost domestic and city waste

Collecting paper for recycling, Friends of the Earth, Avon, UK

▶Add your own ideas to this list.

▶Copy the table opposite. Then add the letters of the ideas and activities that will help improve each environmental area. You may use each letter more than once.

▶Compare and discuss your table with other people's. For at least two of the ideas/activities, discuss in detail how they might help the environment. What problems might be involved?

▶Find out about environmental difficulties like these that may be happening in your own or nearest town or city. Do you think more could be done? If so, what? (See the activity in the Green for Go section in chapter 1.)

The Shenley Lodge Estate, Milton Keynes, UK. Note the energy-efficient houses, the wind generator, solar panels and recycling facilities

Working towards sustainability—Third World

Countries in the Third World have been encouraged to develop along the same lines as the industrialised countries—building large-scale factories, power stations, businesses and so on. But often this form of development has not helped the majority of the countries' people.

More countries are now looking for 'appropriate development', meaning projects which suit the local culture and environment. This kind of development aims to help people help themselves and uses their skills.

Working towards sustainability—international

As well as taking local action, countries will need to work together more closely than ever before. Some progress is already being made. For example:

● Many nations signed the 'Montreal Protocol' in 1987 and 1990. This is an agreement to stop using CFCs by the year 2000 and set up a fund to help Third World countries to switch to alternatives. The European Community has agreed to stop producing CFCs by 1997.

● The International Tropical Timber Agreement, which aims to improve forest management, has been signed.

● The United Nations Environment Programme has developed ten regional seas programmes involving over 120 countries. Where countries share a coastline, they agree to protect their regional sea.

● Certain organisations, such as the World Wide Fund for Nature, have paid off debt in some Third World countries, in return for nature conservation programmes. These are called 'Debt for Nature' swaps.

● The Law of the Sea Convention establishes 200 mile zones around coasts to stop fishing conflicts.

● A series of World Climate Conferences is moving towards agreements on limiting the production of green-·house gases.

● A *World Conservation Strategy* was published in 1980, and a new version called *Caring for the World: A Strategy for Sustainability*, was published in 1991.

● The European Community is toughening its rules on environmental protection, covering such areas as air and water pollution, transport, waste, chemicals and wildlife.

● A number of countries have published their own national conservation strategies or plans.

● In 1987 the World Commission on Environment and Development produced a report on sustainable development called *Our Common Future*.

 ▶**Why did the Commission choose this title?**

Governments meet regularly to discuss progress towards a sustainable world. In Brazil in 1992, children have been invited to put their questions to top politicians.

 ▶**If you were going to this meeting, what questions would you ask?**

Green for go—designing the future

If you've studied this book, you will know that sustainability is based on some key ideas, including:

recycling and reusing materials and waste · making things last · keeping pollution and waste to a minimum · avoiding toxic materials · saving energy · using renewable sources of energy · sharing resources

Over the next thirty years, these ideas are likely to affect many areas of our lives.

▶Taking your house, or house and garden (if you have one), or village or town, think how it may be different in

thirty years' time. What changes might there be? Construct a model or draw a picture to show these changes, and include your own ideas. What ideas could be carried out straight away?

▶ Make up a front page of a newspaper produced in thirty years' time. What sort of environmental stories or 'green' advertisements might it include?

▶ Study 'green claims' for products and services that say they are environmentally friendly. Do you agree with the claims?

▶ Encourage your school to link up with a school in the Third World. Discuss some of the topics you have learnt about in this book by comparing your ideas and experience with your link school.

▶ Encourage your school to 'go green'. A school can conduct an 'environmental audit'—seeing if energy can be saved, and paper and other materials can be recycled. If you set up a recycling scheme, you may be able to save money which can be used to support Third World or environmental charities.

▶ Learn about the work of groups which help the Third World, and become involved if you can.

▶ Write to local and national organisations, authorities and industries involved with using, managing or campaigning for the environment. Learn about areas you are interested in, and become involved in schemes and campaigns to protect the environment.

The global home

For most of this century, people thought that the global environment would look after itself, and could not be harmed by human activity. Now we know this is not true. To make sure of a sustainable and safe Earth, we have to think differently.

People on Earth need to think much more about the environment and the future—and try to ensure that their actions protect both. Nearly everything we do can make a difference. If *we* care for our global environment, *it* will continue to care for our needs and to provide a home for all living things.

To the teacher

The Education Reform Act is changing the ways the curriculum is delivered. Schools are required to undertake a curriculum audit and then formulate their whole curriculum development plans. The result is that attainment targets and programmes of study will be implemented as part of a whole curriculum policy.

'The full potential of the 10 subjects will only be realised if, in curriculum planning, schools seek to identify the considerable overlaps which inevitably exist in both content and in skills. There is in effect an opportunity for schools to carry out content and skills audits. Inter-departmental planning can lead to more coherent development of skills and the reduction of wasted time and overloading caused by duplication of effort.'[1]

We believe this book will help staff to deliver the curriculum.

Attainment targets

The Global Environment presents a cross-curricular approach to Key Stage 3. The book has a much wider perspective than most textbooks in that it takes into account attainment targets and programmes of study from three subject areas (Geography[2], Science[3] and English[4]) as well as the cross-curricular dimensions, skills and themes.

Cross-curricular themes

Apart from the statutory orders relating to subject areas, the Education Reform Act requires schools to take account of cross-curricular themes in the planning and delivery of the curriculum. The themes are an integral part of the whole curriculum and can form a useful curriculum planning tool. This book usefully covers three themes:

Education for Economic and Industrial Understanding: *'It involves controversial issues such as government economic policy and the impact of economic activity on the environment. It prepares pupils for their future economic roles as producers, consumers and citizens.'*[5]

Education for Citizenship includes *'. . . planning—the conflicting demands and pressures, aesthetic, environmental, economic; being a citizen'*, including the *'importance of participating, how to be involved; sources of information'* etc.[6]

Environmental Education *'is concerned with promoting positive and responsible attitudes towards the environment . . . aims to increase pupils' knowledge and understanding of the processes by which environments are shaped; to enable them to recognise both the quality and the vulnerability of different environments; and to help them to identify opportunities for protecting and managing the environment'.*[7]

The chapters

Each chapter explores a key aspect of the global environment and can be used independently of the others. However, pupils following the whole book will build up a stronger understanding of the subject matter and the nature of the issues involved.

The programme of study for Key Stage 3 Geography states: *'An enquiry approach should be adopted for classroom activities.'*[2] This approach is central to the book. Each chapter begins with a challenge, summarising a major current environmental issue. This is followed by 'Your Investigation', which presents questions that are developed in the chapter. The opening section introduces the topic and includes information and activities on the life-support systems of the Earth, meeting certain Science and Geography ATs.

In the next four pages, pupils examine some of the problems and why they are occurring, with examples and case studies from different parts of the world. These pages include some Science ATs and cover aspects of physical and human geography. Additional materials could be used here. These pages are particularly relevant for cross-curricular themes and for English.

The final two pages of each chapter discuss possible solutions at local, national and international levels. The Green for Go activities suggest practical tasks that increase pupils' understanding of issues and help them become involved in solutions.

Concept building

We have written the book to help pupils understand some of the complex environmental issues facing the world today and explore key concepts for the next century—such as global interdependence and sustainability—from ecological, cultural and economic points of view.

Skills development

A key feature of the book is a skills-based approach to learning, which helps pupils develop many of the skills required by National Curriculum attainment targets. These include specific subject skills as well as the cross-curricular dimension, including communication, numeracy, study, problem-solving, personal and social education, and information technology.

Attitudes and values

Throughout the book, pupils are encouraged to empathise with people whose values may be different from theirs. Activities encourage them to express their own attitudes and values, and understand how they are formed, while recognising the validity of different points of view. Each chapter will build their understanding of the ways different societies relate to the world and in particular to the environment.

Active learning

The book is pupil-centred and activity-based. Tasks actively engage pupils in investigations, explorations and speculations through a wide range of active learning techniques including role-play and discussion.

Cooperation and collaboration

Many of the activities in the book are based on pupils working in pairs or small groups. This enables them to take responsibility for their own learning and that of others. The activities aim to encourage discussion and speculation. Research has shown that this style of active learning provides an optimum environment for knowledge retention as well as developing pupils' skills and ability to explore attitudes and values. The National Curriculum has recognised the value of discussion in the learning process and pupils' speaking and listening skills are expected to be assessed in all subjects.

The Global Environment programmes

The IBT series *The Global Environment*, broadcast by BBC School Television (and available on video), covers all the issues raised in this book. It combines spectacular footage from different parts of the world with original filming in Britain and overseas. Although the book can be used independently, the chapters follow the order of the programmes and explore different aspects of the same issues. Pupils who have watched the programmes will find the book more accessible and exciting.

Teachers' notes are available to accompany the programmes. These contain photocopiable active learning materials which help pupils explore the issues further, especially from the point of view of National Curriculum Science. The video of the programmes and the teachers' notes are available from: BBC Educational Publishing, PO Box 234, Wetherby, West Yorkshire LS23 7EU.

We hope your pupils enjoy using the book as much as we have enjoyed writing it.

Sue Lyle and Stephen Sterling

Stephen Sterling was Assistant Director of the Council for Environmental Education until 1986 and now works as a consultant in environmental education. He is Executive Editor of the Annual Review of Environmental Education.

Sue Lyle is a lecturer in primary education at the University of Wales and is the author of several teaching packs, published by Greenlight Publications.

1. Curriculum Guidance 3—The Whole Curriculum, NCC, 1990.
2. Geography in the National Curriculum, HMSO, 1991.
3. National Curriculum, Proposals for Science, DES/Welsh Office, May 1991.
4. English in the National Curriculum (No. 2), HMSO, 1990.
5. Curriculum Guidance 4—Education for Economic and Industrial Understanding, NCC, 1990.
6. Curriculum Guidance 8—Education for Citizenship, NCC, 1990.
7. Curriculum Guidance 7—Environmental Education, NCC, 1990.

Glossary

acid rain rain which has been made acidic through chemical reaction with the products of burning fossil fuels, particularly sulphur dioxide and nitrogen dioxide gases. 'Acid deposition' is a term which also covers acid dust, acid snow and fog as well as acid rain.
aquifer a deposit of porous rocks such as sandstone which holds an underground reservoir of water.

barrage a dam across a watercourse.
biodegraded/biodegradable the ability of material to be broken down by biological means, such as by bacteria. Most materials from natural sources are biodegradable.
biomass the amount of living plant or animal material in a given area, usually expressed by weight. Tropical forests contain large biomass.

canopy the uppermost layers of a forest.
capital the original amount of money borrowed from or deposited in a bank, before *interest* is added. The Earth's natural resources are sometimes called 'environmental capital'.
cash crop crop grown for sale (often abroad) rather than for local consumption.
catalytic converter a device fitted to car exhausts which removes most of the polluting gases. It can only work on a vehicle using unleaded fuel.
climate model a group of theories and predictions about the pattern of climate change and behaviour, based on observations and past evidence.
climatic zones areas of the Earth experiencing a broad type of climate, for example 'tropical zones' or 'temperate zones'.
colonial relating to Britain and other countries having colonies, territories around the world which they ruled.
commercial selling of goods and services, often on a large scale and often for use abroad rather than locally.
coniferous trees of temperate regions which usually have needle-shaped leaves and are usually evergreen, e.g. pines, spruces and firs.
continental shelf a ledge of land extending out from the edge of continents beneath the sea. The shallow coastal waters over continental shelves contain rich sea life, but also receive much more pollution than the deep sea.

debt crisis a situation that grew out of an increase in *international debt* during the 1970s. Vast amounts of money were invested in Western banks as a result of an increase in oil prices. Much of this money was offered to poor countries as loans, but many countries now find that they cannot pay the *interest* on the loans from what they earn from their *exports*.
deciduous trees which shed their leaves annually at the end of the growing season.
deforestation the process of clearing an area of trees.

ecology relationship of organisms with their environment.
ecosystem a community of plants and animals and their environment.
ethanol alcohol.
eviction forced removal of people from land or property that they are occupying.
export to sell abroad; goods sold to other countries.
extractive reserves the untapped supplies of a resource (such as coal) which could be taken out (extracted) and used.

fertile/fertility productive. Fertile soil is rich in nutrients that can support strong growth in plants.
fodder plants grown for animal food.
food chain organisms which are linked by feeding. For example: grass is eaten by a rabbit; the rabbit is eaten by a fox.
fossil fuels fuels formed over millions of years from the remains of plants and animals, in the Earth's crust. Fossil fuels are coal, oil and natural gas.

groundwater water which is found underground, usually in *aquifers*.

hectare a measure of land area. One hectare is equal to 10 000 sq m or 2.471 acres.

import to buy from abroad; goods bought from other countries.
indigenous usually refers to the original inhabitants of a place rather than the people who have come to live there.
industrialised term used to describe the wealthy countries, most of which built up their industries using *raw materials* from the *Third World*. They are sometimes called 'developed countries' or 'the North' (most, though not all, are north of the equator).
Industrial Revolution term used to describe the transformation from a rural to an industrial society that took place during the nineteenth century in the countries now known as *industrialised*.
infrastructure supporting structure. A city's infrastructure can include roads, transport, electricity, waterworks etc.
interest a regular payment made on a loan. It is usually a fixed percentage of the total loan that is owed to the lender in addition to the *capital* (see also *debt crisis* and *international debt*).
international debt money owed to the industrialised countries and Western banks, mostly by *Third World* countries. Many poor countries get into debt because they cannot pay the high cost of *imports* from the low price they receive for their *exports*. Often they are lent more money to develop their exports and pay the *interest* on the money they have already borrowed (see *debt crisis*).

international market not an actual place, but the idea of countries competing against each other to find buyers for their products or *exports*.

landfill site a hole or excavated area used for dumping waste, usually controlled by waste disposal authorities. The best sites are lined, and covered daily, but old sites were often unlined and can leak toxic liquids into the groundwater.

leaching the process by which water washes minerals down through soil, or out into streams.

life-support systems all the systems on Earth which allow life to be sustained.

lumber logs and sawn timber.

marginal on the edge. Marginal land is poor land, often unsuitable for farming, which may literally be 'on the edge' of better land, or 'on the edge' of being worthwhile to cultivate or graze.

nutrients the mineral substances that a plant takes up through its roots for food; any nourishing substance.

organic relating to or derived from plants and animals. Organic growing is agriculture or horticulture which relies on fertilisers from animal and plant sources, and natural control methods rather than chemically based pesticides.

pastoralist a farmer who makes a living by grazing animals.

photosynthesis the process by which leaves make plant food (carbohydrate) from water, carbon dioxide taken from the air and the energy of sunlight.

raw materials natural substances that are usually grown or mined in order to be made into something else or 'processed'.

recharge replenish or refill (water supplies).

recycle using materials or energy again after a first use, sometimes in a different form, or for a different purpose.

renewable/non-renewable renewable resources are those which are able to replace or renew themselves, such as timber, fish and soil, or an energy source that will never run out, such as the sun and wind power. Non-renewable resources are those which take such a long time to form, they are regarded as unable to replace themselves. Coal, oil, copper and tin are examples of non-renewable resources. It is important to conserve non-renewable resources, and use renewable resources no faster than they can replace themselves.

residues agricultural chemicals which remain on food after processing and may be eaten.

resource something which can be used and useful, for example land, minerals, energy and labour.

salinated/salinisation salinated ground is ground which contains a high level of salts. Salinisation is the process of becoming salty, often caused by poor irrigation methods.

shanty town area, usually on the outskirts of a city, where poor people build their own homes, often without basic services such as running water, sewers and electricity.

sludge the waste sewage material which is left after processing by a sewage works.

squatters people who settle on land (or property) that does not legally belong to them.

sustainable/sustainably using resources carefully so that they are available to meet people's needs today and in the future, without damaging the environment.

sustainable development using and developing the Earth's resources and environments carefully so that they can provide for the basic needs of all people, and also provide for the needs of future generations.

temperate temperate areas are those lying in the mid-latitudes of the Earth, between tropical and polar regions. Temperate forest grows in these regions.

Third World term used to describe the economically poor countries, sometimes referred to as 'developing countries' or 'the South' (most, though not all, are south of the equator). None of these terms are totally accurate (see also *industrialised* countries).

transnational companies companies that operate in different parts of the world using local workers, but whose owners are usually from the industrialised countries.

water cycle the circulation of the Earth's water between atmosphere, land and sea, through rainfall, river flow, evaporation and plant transpiration.

water-logging the process of becoming saturated or completely soaked with water.

water table the surface of a water-soaked layer of rock underground. A well will only provide water if it reaches the water table.

Resources

For teachers
Teaching material

Brian Milner, *The Global Environment*, Students' Activities and Teachers' Notes, BBC Educational Publishing/IBT, 1990. Accompanies the IBT/BBC School TV series. Emphasis on National Curriculum Science.

David Hicks, Miriam Steiner, *Making Global Connections: a World Studies Workbook*, Oliver and Boyd, 1989.

Roy Williams, *One Earth, Many Worlds*, WWF, 1989. A cross-curricular approach to teaching and learning about global environmental issues.

Sue Greig, Graham Pike, David Selby, *Earthrights*, WWF/Kogan Page, 1987.

Sue Lyle, Maggie Roberts, *A Mountain Child. A Rainforest Child. An Arctic Child*, Greenlight Publications. Three active-learning packs.

Sue Lyle, Maggie Roberts, *Forest Matters: Global Concerns and Environmental Perspectives*, Greenlight Publications, 1990. A skills-based learning pack on environmental issues.

David Wright, *The Greenhouse Effect*, WWF, 1990. Teaching pack, video and poster.

City Lights: Fatal Attractions?, WWF, 1990. Teachers' notes and student resources on urbanisation.

Briefing material

Lester Brown *et al.*, *State of the World* reports, Worldwatch Institute/Unwin Hyman. Reports on key environment/development issues. Produced yearly.

Joni Seager (ed.), *The State of the Earth*, Unwin Hyman, 1990. An atlas of environmental issues.

Geoffrey Lean, Don Hinrichsen, Adam Markham, *Atlas of the Environment*, WWF/Arrow Books, 1990. Detailed maps and articles on many aspects of the environment and development.

Lloyd Timberlake, Laura Thomas, *When the Bough Breaks—Our Children, Our Environment*, Earthscan, 1990. A reader on the effect of underdevelopment and environmental issues on the world's children.

Edward Goldsmith, Nicholas Hildyard (eds.), *The Earth Report 2*. Short articles on key global environmental issues.

For young people
Books

John Baines, *Acid Rain*, Wayland, 1989.

John Baines, *Protecting the Oceans*, Wayland, 1989.

Ewan McLeish, *The Spread of Deserts*, Wayland, 1990.

Barbara James, *Waste and Recycling*, Wayland, 1990.

John Becklake, *The Climate Crisis*, Franklin Watts, 1989.

Martin Banks, *Conserving the Rainforests*, Wayland, 1989.

Nick Middleton, *Atlas of Environmental Issues*, Oxford University Press, 1988.

Alisdair Rogers, *Atlas of Social Issues*, Oxford University Press, 1990.

Philip Parker, *Water for Life*, Simon and Schuster, 1991.

Richard Spurgeon, *Ecology—a Practical Introduction with Projects and Activities*, Usborne, 1988.

'Spaceship Earth' series—cartoon-style aproach to environmental themes, Cassell, 1990. Titles include: Steve Skidmore, *Poison! Beware!*; Steve Skidmore, *What a Load of Rubbish*; Thompson Yardley, *Down the Plughole*.

David Day, Michael McPartland, *Down to Earth—the Environment and the Way we Live in it*, Lion Educational, 1990.

Debbie Silver, Bernadette Vallely, *The Young Person's Guide to Saving the Planet*, Virago, 1990.

Marianne Frances, *Small Change—a Pocketful of Practical Actions to Help the Environment*, The Centre for Human Ecology, Edinburgh, 1989.

Organisations
(for information and advice on action)

World Wide Fund for Nature (WWF), Panda House, Weyside Park, Godalming, Surrey GU7 1XR.

WATCH Trust for Environmental Education, 22 The Green, Nettleham, Lincoln LN2 2NR (*On Stream* pollution survey pack, see page 29).

Oxfam, 274 Banbury Road, Oxford OX2 7DZ.

Friends of the Earth, 26–28 Underwood Street, London N1 7JU.

British Trust for Conservation Volunteers, 36 St Mary's St, Wallingford, Oxfordshire OX10 0EU.

Marine Conservation Society, 9 Gloucester Road, Ross-on-Wye, Herefordshire HR9 5BU.

National Society for Clean Air and Environmental Protection, 136 North Street, Brighton BN1 1RG.

Youth TAG (Technology Action Group), Intermediate Technology, Myson House, Railway Terrace, Rugby CV21 3HT.

Aluminium Can Recycling Association, 1 Mex House, 52 Blucher Street, Birmingham B1 1QU.

Department of the Environment, Room A302, Romney House, 43 Marsham Street, London SW1P 3PY.